PK

The Tragedy and Triumph
of Growing Up as a Pastor's Kid

Rob Litzinger

Cover design by Jason Francia. Cover photo by Amber Litzinger, Copyright 2011 Joyful Life Photography. Cover model: Dan Litzinger.

To my mom and dad who never really succeeded at pastoring, but raised three boys who would all at some point be in full time ministry. Something worked. To my wife's parents who poured their lives into their sons-in-law and raised girls that love God, love people. To those who patiently mentored me throughout my life, offering discipline and great advice ... mentors saved my life.

For many years I felt the deep conviction that my story had greater meaning. I'm passionate about this story because really, it's His Story that I get to live. I knew I needed to get it written down and get it into the hands of those who needed to hear the heartache and the hope of my life. But I don't like to write. So how does someone who isn't a writer end up writing a book? One word: people.

I'd like to thank my wife for her unending support of me and my passion. I love walking together with you, Cindy. I couldn't have done it without you. Thanks to my kids, Andrew, India, Jenn, Kaley, Lacey, and Torey for allowing me the extra time it took to finally get these thoughts onto paper. I love all of you.

Next is the team of many volunteers who edited, revised, and shaped this book from rough ideas and sermon notes into a book that I hope brings you, the reader, on a journey from hurt to healing. Thanks to my hard working editors: Dan Theisen, Tara Brown and LeeAnn Perelli-Minetti. You actually like to do that stuff? Amazing!

And I can't say enough about my church family. Thanks to my elder team, pastoral care team, apprentices, ministry leaders, and all of the servants who make running a busy, growing church possible. At Church for Life, we love doing LIFE together!

And last of all, thank, you, Jesus for loving me even when I didn't love Your bride.

When I think about where I am today, sometimes it's hard to believe that it is me. The fact that I have an amazing marriage—a miracle. The fact that I love people—a miracle. The fact that I love church people—a miracle beyond belief. The fact that all three Litzinger boys have been in full-time ministry, serving God, serving His church—humbling.

My main goal is to write to the pastor's kid who suffered like I did. I am primarily sharing my story to help them, but some of the suffering I endured is universal. We all struggle with things from our pasts and must overcome our own fears and faults. So, whether you're a PK or not, this story will change your heart if you are brave enough to read it.

In the following pages, I will tell my story as distinctly as I can remember it. I am not a writer. I am actually not much of a reader either (although I force myself to be). Yet every time I met a PK and saw the struggle inside, my heart began to do something that for a long time I didn't understand. I believe I have been called to specifically work with PKs. I have known for years there is something in me I can use to help PKs, but getting it out has been hard—harder than I thought.

If I can set out one clean glass of fresh water for you before we start, it is this: I believe there is a special destiny for pastor's kids … but it is oh-so-hard to grab. Not because we *can't* see, but because of what we **have** seen.

For every reader out there, PK or not, I pray this personal note will take your experience from a liability to an asset, understanding:

*"This is the message we have heard from Him and declare to you: God is light; **in Him there is no darkness at all.**"*

1 John 1:5 (NIV)

People began to sit on different sides of the church. It got that bad. One side liked my dad, and the other did not. We all knew that. My dad tried his hardest; he about killed himself trying to please everyone, trying to be as humble as possible so people would be cool. But this Sunday night, it was not cool. They had called in the conference president to speak.

The night before, we'd had a meeting in the musty, dark basement normally reserved for kid's church. It felt like more of a dungeon that night. At 15 years old, I demanded to go. I wanted to protect my dad in the worst way. I didn't want to see that look of hurt on his face again. I didn't want to deal with the three days of darkness and depression that would descend on our house after a meeting like this. Amazingly, I was convincing enough that my parents let me go.

The "sheep" complained about my dad's leaving the outside light on all night at the church-owned house we had the "privilege" of living in. They said he was wasting precious church resources. My brother worked late until two or three in the morning and Dad left the light on for him. They didn't care. They complained about his reading and referring to newspaper articles or current events out of magazines. "Read the Word. That's all we need. We can read the paper at home," they would say. They also complained about my job at a call center where we took orders for many companies, some of which they didn't think were "good companies."

On and on they went, complaint after complaint, until my dad looked totally defeated.

He had his hands folded on his lap, looking at the floor. Mom sat with a tissue in her hand, her shoulders slumped, trying not make eye contact.

No one stood up for him. No one came to his rescue. I wanted to. I wanted to tear into this bunch of Pharisees. I was seething, but I didn't protect my dad … no one did.

See, I had said something once before. When I was seven or eight, I used to stand by the back door with dad as he greeted all the people as they left the service. There was an unspoken rule. The service would go **no more** than one hour exactly. One Wednesday night, my dad had a particularly fun message. He was in good humor, feeling good. I loved him like that. It wasn't too often those days though. Since he really got into the message, he went a bit long—maybe 10 minutes over.

He was still feeling good as he stood by the back door; then it happened. One of the old ladies walked up, tapped her watch and said, "You just can't do it, can you? You just can't seem to end on time."

I saw my dad's face fall, as a look of defeat overcame him … and I snapped. I began to scream, "I hate you, you old biddie! I hate you! I hate all of you!" I was crying and yelling, blubbering.

My dad swooped me up and ran me outside and began to cry with me. "Rob, we can't do this. We can't act this way. You can't say things like that. I'm so sorry, Rob. I'm sorry."

As I have contemplated over the years, I think that was the moment—the moment when I declared in my little heart, "I hate
the church. I hate church people, and as long as I live, I will
never put myself in the position of being taken advantage of."
The vow I made that night would take many years, many men-
toring hours, and the supernatural work of the Holy Spirit to
break. Even with all of the work that has gone on inside me,
this is still my number one core fear today: the fear of being
taken advantage of.

*The vow I made that night would take
many years… and the Holy Spirit to break.*

I stand guard against this fear every day. I find myself spending
hours driving around town to all the office stores, checking the
internet, looking at all the sale flyers … just to save $10. If I cal-
culated my hourly time, I figure I have wasted about $300 trying
to save $10. This vow I made as a little boy still affects both the
things I do and decisions I make. These little vows continue to
wreak havoc throughout life.

QUESTIONS:

• What vows or firm decisions have you made along the way in
your journey?

• How are those vows or decisions affecting you today?

- Are you being held captive by decisions you made out of self-protection?

- When are you going to break free?

- What crazy statement(s) have you spoken that still might be affecting your decisions?

We left the meeting where everyone had complained, and I never said one word. I had been "trained better." I walked out, having left my dad without backup. I felt guilty and ashamed. I should have rocked those people's worlds, yet then I would be like them, wouldn't I? My dad crawled into the comfort of his darkness, retreating away from my brothers and me, from my mom, and from the world. He was not even mad, just hurt. He had given everything, and it wasn't enough.

We chatted with the conference president that night, and he said the people were wrong. So why didn't **he** say anything? Why didn't **he** defend my dad? I began to mistrust leadership and authority.

To this day, my mom and dad still will not talk about what happened next. The conference president stood at the pulpit for the Sunday night service and said, "Tonight we will break bread and offer forgiveness to one another and begin the process of healing this church."

Now I still don't know who spoke first, but before I knew it, people were yelling, accusing, and talking bad about my dad. One side was defending him ... while the other was accusing him of the stupidest things. These things were nothing sinful, just petty. Some were lies, such as my dad was not making his required monthly visits to their homes. My mom started to cry, which she rarely **ever** did. My brothers and I began to cry. Our dad was being ripped apart in public, right in front of us. He had stood up to try and defend himself and was being shouted down. Mom grabbed our hands and dragged us to the altar, saying through her sobs, "Pray, boys! Just pray!" We **did** pray.

As we knelt at the altar, all I could hear was my mom's wailing and my dad's trying to defend himself. I felt so helpless. Darkness was filling my heart. I **hated** these people. We prayed the fire that fell on the grumbling Israelites would consume these people behind us. We prayed these people would die.

That night, over half the church stormed out and never came back. My dad was never the same. Years before this happened, I remember my dad as funny, dynamic, and friendly. He was my hero, a man of faith who lived his life in service to the King of Kings, caring for the people around him. He would carry their burdens with them when they met with tough times. He preached with energy and enthusiasm from the front of the church. He was living his life in humble submission to Jesus, showing others the way they could have a great relationship with their Savior as well.

Our church robbed him of all of that. When we were kids, on one Wednesday of every year, we—the pastor and his family—stayed home while the rest of the people went to church and voted on us. Afterwards, some pitiful old lady would stop by and give us the thumbs up or the thumbs down.

We lived under a microscope. The congregation watched our every move; some of them even shared our backyard. What could have been respectful accountability became invasion and intrusion into our daily lives. Dad's position as the pastor was at the whim and mercy of the congregation and board. If they didn't like what he was telling them, we'd all lose our home, our friends, our neighbors—everything.

Looking back, it is no surprise he fell into the funk that he still lives in today. We had a tent in the backyard that we had set up to play in. One day, I looked outside; my dad was in there, just hiding from the world. Soon after that, he walked away from ministry saying, "You couldn't pay me a million dollars to preach." All he wanted to do was build a house in the middle of cornfields where you couldn't see anyone and didn't have any neighbors. That's exactly what they did. It's where they live today in Ohio. My wife, kids, and I recently visited them. We were just *there*. The corn was 12 feet high on all four sides of their acreage. There were no people and no sounds. They were there just hiding in their hurts. My dad is a shell of the man he used to be.

One thing I knew: I loved God, but I hated His people.

One thing I knew: I loved God, but I hated His people. My brothers and I used to say, "If it's preach or go to hell, that's an easy one." We usually left the rest unsaid.

It is a miracle of grace that both of my brothers now attend and serve at Church for Life where I pastor today. As I tell these stories in my messages or in our leadership classes, my brothers tell me they have pushed these events down so far, they have forgotten them. Even so, the toxins are still there, seeping through in everything we do. We have all had our journeys of restoration, but God has been good to us, walking us to healing and healthy productive ground again.

He *is* a good shepherd, and He *will* lead us into green pastures and beside still waters.

QUESTIONS:

• How have you been hurt as a Pastor's Kid?

• How have your past experiences affected your relationships with others?

• If you have, when did you begin to get cynical?

• Was there a moment when darkness flooded your heart?

• Have you found yourself acting in ways that you don't like, but feel unable to stop?

It was with a bitter and broken heart I entered the "big world." Except for kindergarten and one year in a Christian school, we were homeschooled. I had just turned 18, and as much as I loved my mom and dad … I couldn't stay. I moved 11 hours away from New York to Ohio. I cried for three days when my parents left me in Ohio. I didn't know until years later that my mom and dad had to pull over just out of sight because they were crying so hard.

My childhood had been a good, loving, caring time; yet it had been hard too. My dad wasn't the same; he has still never recovered. Still to this day, my mom shakes when we talk about past church issues or when some kind of conflict arises.

But there I was now, on my own. I was now responsible for my own life. I left home as soon as I could. Even now, my dad asks, "Why did you have to leave so quickly?" I had a great relationship with my mom and dad; I just couldn't stand being around all those church people any more. I was afraid I would end up defeated like my dad; or worse, God would call me to follow in my dad's footstep and become a pastor. So I fled. I moved a long day's drive away, near Columbus, Ohio. I bought *my* own place and began to fight for *my* vision for *my* life.

I was going to go to Ohio State University, become a lawyer, and fight everybody in the world I didn't agree with. I really wanted to fight for God, but the desire was out of justice and anger … not mercy.

I subscribed to the Christian Law Association newsletter, listened to every political debate I could, and began my ***personal*** conquest to right every wrong in the world.

A simple word for it was ***arrogance***.

I argued with everyone about everything. I brought up every explosive subject you could think of and was armed with so much information that I could run circles around most people who bit on my toxic, shiny little fishing lure. I honed my skills, sharpened my tongue, and, like Saul in the New Testament, harassed, stabbed, and killed people with my words "all in the name of God."

In reality, I was acting like a jerk, even siding with Satan. I was trying my best to protect myself and ensure that no one could put me in a place where I would be at his mercy like my dad had been.

> *You can't change your history*
> *until you've come to grips with*
> *your story*

The better I got at it, the more arrogant I became. I told myself, "I will never let myself be beaten by anyone, no matter what the cost." I took it ***way*** too far, ruined many relationships, and isolated myself from so many people. Worst of all, I was a terrible reflection of Christ. It was all rooted in a vow I made that one Wednesday night after church when some old lady accosted my dad. So I vowed: I will ***never*** let myself be taken advantage of.

You can't change your history until you've come to grips with your story. This is the reason I have told my story over the years. So many people have identified with my story and shared one of their own, including my brothers.

· *The PK whose dad walked away from the church and from her mom after building a beautiful building*

· *The PK whose dad was a raging tyrant at home, but at church was the "fire" that everybody looked for—just plain wasted of energy and life*

· *The PKs whose dads, like mine, did their best, and their best just wasn't good enough*

My dad failed and accepted defeat as the only option and sowed defeat into the next generation. This was not a generational curse, but a generational negative faith seed.

There are a lot of people out there with faith; it's just negative faith. It is still **believing** in something that they can't see … but it's always bad stuff! God's faith is believing in something that you can't see yet that is good! Negative faith people can always see bad things ahead. They can drag down the strongest workhorse. But we who have faith in Jesus can always see good things out ahead. The hard part is the transition from being a bad news Christian to a good news Christian. It is two different worlds.

But not until you process **your** story can you find freedom to change the **history** you are making today. You must first reconcile with the story of yesterday.

At this point, maybe you are feeling a bit the way I am feeling while writing this. It is feeling pretty heavy, and, frankly, a bit hopeless. You can sense how dark these times were for our family. Maybe you've had your own dark times.

Let me give you motivation to read on to the final chapters. ***This is the whole reason Jesus came!*** He knew life would be tough, that we would get hurt, and we would need to be rescued … we would at some point need answers. He has answered those questions for me, and He will for you too. Read on.

QUESTIONS:

- What questions do you have for Jesus?

- What pain do you want him to heal?

- What lifeless growths do you need him to amputate?

- Where are you on this transition from negative faith to positive faith?

I was about six years old when the Christian school we were connected with had a "what-do-you-want-to-be-when-you-grow-up" day. Some kids were there in nurses' uniforms, while others had their dad's tool belts on. I saw doctor's stethoscopes, aprons, and chef's hats. Yet, there I was ... my hair slicked back, wearing a three-piece, with a *big* Bible under my arm. Yes, I even had the matching vest. I marched up to the microphone and announced, "I am going to be a preacher like my dad!" How did I go from innocence to the bitterness and mistrust I felt at 18?

One word: People.

At Church for Life, you will hear us talk a lot about living in "the default." I believe 90% of people live there. What's the default? It is the natural place we all go when we live unchecked by our spirits. It is when we live by our feelings and emotions. In electronics lingo, it's the path of least resistance. That is the default and the place where most people live. There is a default for everything—for friendships, for organizations, our minds, our diets, exercise, and yes, churches. The default is the lowest common denominator in us as human beings. When people meet and congregate at this low place of default, it is disaster. You get gangs and horrible marriages. Many couples are coming together at a place of default, leading to destruction. The default creates churches and groups of friends who are bad for each other. Codependent relationships are simply relationships that are forged by coming together at a default.

The Bible addresses this default as "flesh" or "humanity"; God actually sent His own Son to save us from this default. This default is why we need the Gospel. This is why it's good news! There are bad news churches and good news churches. Church for Life is a good news church! The good news is that there is an answer for people living in the default—the natural lowest place to live. If you are reading this book, then you are probably ready to break out of the default! Welcome to supernatural growth!

Ohio State didn't work out. I sat down with a counselor, and she told me by the time I graduated, I would probably have close to $100,000 in school debt! I was shocked and really couldn't stand the thought of starting my life with that much debt. I needed options. I sold the little place I had bought and moved in with my uncle and aunt. I was stressed out and desperate to get life my moving. I have always been a decision-making, driven person, and sitting around with no clear direction for my life was driving me nuts.

One morning, while I was lying on the floor in my sleeping bag, God spoke to me, saying to go see a military recruiter. What? That was **definitely** not in my plan. My plan was to take on everyone who disagreed with me for the glory of Rob through becoming a lawyer. *I* wanted to do the commanding. With people yelling at me and telling me what to do, could I handle it?

That morning, without telling anybody, I looked up the local recruiters and went to see them. The Marines were first. I thought I might as well go all out! The guy was an idiot, pushy and loud. Next was the Air Force. I met a really nice recruiter who asked a lot of questions about my life. He gave me some great advice, and as far as I can tell, never lied to me once. He was a Christian, and, to this day, I know it was a divine appointment. Within a few days, I was signed up to join the United States Air Force.

Mom and Dad were scared; it was 1991 and Desert Storm had just kicked off in Iraq. I just knew this was God. The Air Force would pay for my college, so I could still get to my plan of becoming a lawyer and righting every wrong in the world. The difference was Uncle Sam would pay for it.

I shipped off to Lackland Air Force Base in Texas and jumped into the intense life of basic training. My recruiter gave me several bits of good advice. He said, "Don't be first. Don't be last. Don't get noticed. Stay right in the middle of everything. Try and just blend in and do what they tell you to do." That didn't happen.

God loves you enough to not let you marinate in the default if you will follow Him!

As I did my stuff with intensity and perfection, my training instructor noticed. Pretty soon, she put guys who didn't deserve to graduate on either side of me. She said simply, "If either of them fail, you fail." Not cool! My fear of being taken advantage of spiked. Not fair! So I forbade the guys to touch anything they owned; I did mine *and* theirs. I ironed the six by six inch T-shirts three times. I made tight beds three times; I actually physically pushed them while they ran. And then, I got dorm guard duty all night for seething about it.

God loves you enough to not let you marinate in the default if you will follow Him! Here I was in basic training, a place I thought even God wouldn't like, and He was there. He was working details to deal with my defaults and my core fears. He was there to poke the areas where I was tender so I knew I was sick.

I got those guys through and didn't lose either of them. Finally, the week came before graduation when you get handed your first set of orders. Exciting! They let you fill out a "dream sheet," and, because I grew up in New York, I put in for all the bases back East: New York, Pennsylvania, even Connecticut. As I tore open my orders, I looked and saw "MT." MT, where was MT? I think I might have even asked someone … MT? Montana? Where was that? I got back to my bunk and looked in the back of a notebook for a US map. Way up north, way out west was this state called Montana. The farthest west I had been was Indiana. What I saw was almost in Canada, sparse with small, little cities.

Montana—I couldn't picture it; it was too far away. That didn't fit into my plan! I had heard the briefing about being able to switch orders in the first 48 hours, so I began to circulate, asking if there were any others with my same specialty who wanted to go to Montana. Of the 50 guys in our flight, I found one who was going to Whiteman Air Force Base in Missouri who would trade. I was excited, and so was he. We got the paperwork and began to fill it out to make the switch. That night as I lay there, with 25 other guys sniffing, talking in their sleep, and snoring … God began to speak to me—through a simple whisper—"That is not where I sent you."

QUESTIONS:

- Are you living in the default, the lowest common denominator, in an area of your life?

- Are you surrounding yourself with "default people" who are at the same place you are, with no one to make you think bigger, or drag you out of your humanity?

- How will you make sure you are not one of the common 90% who are stuck?

- How are *you* going to become a 10-percenter?

- Are you part of a good news church?

One thing I have learned in going on 20 years of ministry is there are **always** exit ramps **right before** destiny. I see it over and over, and many people take them. They get desperate for destiny, and, like Adam and Eve, try and take a shortcut to a place that looks good to them. PK, listen. This is where most of those people who gave our dads a hard time live, which is why they can't stand progress, change, or momentum! They are stuck. For some of you, this is where your dad lived or lives, taking the exit ramp almost within sight of destiny **every time!** I am writing this book to help those of you who have witnessed so much "stuckness" snap out of the counterfeit ramp of destruction. Just keep following Jesus … it's close. He's close by … and He has some **serious** momentum!

I wrestled with those words all night … "That is not where I sent you."

Fortunately, I listened. In the morning, I found the other kid and just straight-up without emotion told him that I could not switch with him. He was **mad**. He had dreamt about hunting in Montana all night. Many times, I looked back at the simple, tiny, small decision and shudder when I think: my wife was there, my life was there, my first mentors were there … my destiny was there in Great Falls, Montana. I **almost** missed it. Where would I be today? Would I have been one of those old bald dudes still living in the dorms at 40 because life just hadn't happened yet? Thank you, Holy Spirit! I had one more stop to make before heading to what seemed like Egypt: my tech school.

My tech school ended up being at Chanute Air Force Base in Rantoul, Illinois, in between no-where and corn fields. I spent eight months there. Every Friday night, buses would line up in front of the dorms and bus the guys and girls into the clubs in the nearby city of Champaign. I would watch and hear them, but go sit in my room, unwilling to participate in the sin that followed. So, lonely, I went down to the day room, where, for the first time, I watched television.

I haven't mentioned until now that I grew up Holiness/Mennonite. If you don't know what that is, think a little bit more chilled-out Amish. This meant no TV, no secular radio, no sports, no short sleeves, and no clothes that were in style. Those things meant trying to be like the world. Women wore long dresses and never cut their hair. We had to wear long sleeve shirts under our polos that Burger King gave us to wear to work. Most of us were homeschooled and sheltered. Mom would kick kids out of our yard if they came over with shorts on. Needless to say, between the homeschooling and the weirdness of our belief system, we didn't have many friends growing up. So here I was in the middle of nowhere, with nowhere to go sitting in my room by myself **again**. I told myself, "I'm used to it; I can do this."

So on those nights, I began to watch TV. China Beach was in reruns and I fell in love with Dana Delaney. Trust me, if you have **never** watched TV or a movie, it is very real when you do for the first time. It's believable and incredibly striking. Kids today grow up pretty dull about what's on the screen, but for me it was an incredible experience. I kinda lived out Vietnam for a few months through that first TV show, while the guys would come back, puking in my toilet in the middle of the night and hungover the next morning. Husbands were cheating on wives. Wives were planning for divorces when they got home. It was a sad introduction into the world I had been sheltered from. Seeing lives wasted and living in the default became ever so clear. It was close to the bottom of life.

QUESTIONS:

- Have you taken an exit ramp right before destiny? When?

- In what ways as a PK, were you different from everyone else? How did this make you feel?

- When God speaks, do you hear Him? Are you listening?

- When you do, are you obeying Him or ignoring Him?

My parents searched for a Holiness church that would come pick me up. They found one about an **hour** away that said they would send a couple to come get me on Sundays. As I stood by the front gate of the base, an older couple pulled up in a big conversion van. They picked me up Sunday morning, then invited me for dinner. After I ate with them, they showed me to a boy's room to take a customary "Sunday afternoon nap." Afterwards I went back to church with them for the evening service.

What I didn't know until later is they had a son my age who was killed by a drunk driver. For eight months, that couple took me in, loved on me, cooked me meals every Sunday, and built an atmosphere for me all those guys and girls in the dorms could only try to create by partying and drinking. I had a **family**.

I believe the power of the church to serve the world is vastly underestimated.

The church was another story. The pastor was legalistic, harsh, mean to his wife, and believed you should have as many kids as you possibly can. I didn't get much from him, except another bad experience with the Church. But that couple … I will never forget them. Don't forget to reach out to lonely people. Just a meal, a little love, and a room can change a life. It changed mine.

I believe the power of the church to serve the world is **vastly** underestimated. If believers would open their homes, their resources, and their lives to the world around them, the church would be the greatest asset that has ever been given to the world besides Jesus. PK, we have the ability to **get this** more than the average person. We have the capability to harness this gift to the world called the church. I will show you how to access what you have seen, heard and been a part of your whole life. PKs have a unique ability and perspective gained from living a unique life in a unique home … a pastor's home. You may not see it yet. Let's walk together for a while here and go together. Come with me, and I will show it to you.

As I left Chanute Air Force Base, Illinois, for the long drive to Great Falls, Montana, the Air Force gave me four days to get there. On the way, I stopped by Mount Rushmore, the Badlands, and some of the other tourist traps. As I sat for those long hours of driving alone, I began to ask myself, "What am I doing? How does this get me anywhere? Am I just wasting four years of my life?" The lies of the Enemy hit me hard while I was unprotected, in between church families with no one around to check my thoughts. I was headed to the middle of nowhere … again, and I was pretty sure I just might have made another mistake.

After driving across a vast flat plain, the road dropped toward the Missouri River, and I saw the city of Great Falls, Montana, where I would be spending the next four years of my life. You could see the whole city in one look at the top of the hill from end to end. Where the town ended, vast fields of wheat started. Mountain ranges were on two sides and then prairie beyond that … for hundreds of miles. I got to my dorm at Malmstrom Air Force Base, settled in with a roommate I had never met, and started on-the-job training.

As a missile technician, my job was working with nuclear weapons. At that time, there were 200 ICBMs (Intercontinental Ballistic Missiles) around Malmstrom. Each missile could make it to Russia in under 30 minutes. I started in the tool room like everyone did and worked 12 to 12 everyday—either midnight to noon or noon to midnight. This made it tough to do much. Again, I was lonely in the wilderness, living with 260 people in this dorm—mostly guys—with two to a room with a joint bathroom. I came home most days to guys' watching porn in my room, or woke up at night to my roommate's having sex with his girlfriend four feet away from me, who also had a collection of about 60 Playboy magazines beside the toilet. This was going to be tough.

I would try and escape to the day room, but all that was ever on was HBO or MTV. Neither was good for me. This was a hostile world, and I didn't know what to do. One day, I went to the local mall. I was used to the three-story galleria malls in New York always full of people. This mall was empty; the stores were all open though. So finally, I went in to one of the stores and asked the cashier, "Is … the mall open?"

"Yes," she said with a weird look.

"So … where are all the people?" I asked her.

Her response was a wake-up call for me. "Oh, this is the way it always is during the day … empty." I thought, *I am **never** going to find a girl here! This place is close to the end of the world!* I was starting to get a bad feeling about all of this.

The amazing thing was that my dorm had all the guys with top secret clearances who were certified to work with nuclear weapons. This dorm was a cut above the rest. I heard amazing stories about what went on in the other dorms where no one had the security clearances we did. I began to run, play racquetball, ride my bike—anything to get out of that environment. I had to find a better group of people to become part of. The schedule I was working made it hard to get out or to find a church, but I had to. My parents had put that foundation in me.

> *One thing no one can really escape from:*
> *You must do the right thing to get the*
> *right results.*

One thing no one can really escape from is this: You must do the right thing in order to get the right results. No matter your hang-ups, no matter your past, no matter what anyone did to you … **you** are still responsible for the seed you personally sow. And whatever seed you sow is what you will harvest or collect. The fact is I really despised the church, but I despised sin, partying, and random sex more. When we had a weekend break in basic training and all the married guys and girls were all planning to get hotel rooms and "hook up" for the night, I knew as bad as I felt the church had been to me … it was still better than carnage. I don't know how many people blew up their marriages that weekend, but what I witnessed was a complete lack of any self-control.

QUESTIONS:

- Who has been a positive influence on your life?

- How have you responded when surrounded with sin?

- What kind of seed have you planted? What kind of crop are you expecting?

- When have you fought temptation and won? When have you given in?

Now I was in the position of either joining the party scene or finding something better. There was no one to blame here; I was on my own. If I sowed the wrong seed now, I would get the wrong kind of harvest. Sin was always right there, crouching at my door. I didn't always win either.

The guy in the room next to me was a Christian too, and one day he said, "You know those Playboys by the toilet? Are you struggling with looking at them like I am?"

"Yeah," I said, "I have been." He didn't know what to do, but I did. I went and grabbed half the stack and told him to grab the other half. We walked them out to the dumpster and threw them in. Mission accomplished. My roommate who owned the magazines was seething for the next couple of days, but didn't ever say anything.

These were defining moments for me—choosing the right thing over the default. The default was looking at those magazines; what came along with that is not too hard to figure out. I knew if I didn't find better company, I would begin to absorb the path of least resistance and begin to walk towards the default. So I decided right away to find a church. I would work from midnight to 10 a.m., take a late lunch break, jump into some clothes or just go in my uniform, and try churches.

I was lonely, and I was determined to find a good group of people. I tried with no luck to find a church like the one I grew up in, so I tried the Nazarene church first. I walked in, sat in the back, did the service which included a time of greeting, and not one person ever came to talk to me. This happened in five different churches! I would leave lonelier than when I had come. Everyone would get in their little huddles, and there I was, almost desperate for a little healthy conversation; no one even cared enough to come and talk.

This is why our church in Santa Maria, California, is known as sometimes an overwhelmingly friendly church; we work hard on that every Sunday. I have had grumpy people even get mad when they have visited about being "mobbed" by people before, after, and during the break of the service. We pound this into our vision, because I was the guy on the back row. I figure after the second or third week at our church, you now have a responsibility to walk around and get to know people. We have host teams out in the parking lot, welcome teams at the doors, hospitality teams setting up two stations of donuts and coffee, and ushers helping seat and serve you. We don't fool around with this, because we *know* how valuable it is. I learned that lesson at my next church visit.

I was listening to the Christian radio when I heard a concert advertized at a "Christian center." I didn't know if it was a church or some kind of Christian community center, but I decided a Christian concert might be good for me. So I found the address, and off I went.

As I walked up to the metal warehouse, I didn't even suspect a church was inside. To me, a church was a small square building with a steeple, and even a bell inside, or at least a set of speakers hooked to a cassette player with bells recorded. However, this stark, metal building fit my idea that it was a community center.

As I walked through the front doors and saw concrete floors, metal walls and mauve fabric-covered chairs, I was greeted by loud, vivacious girl who said, "Hey!!!" and gave me a **huge** hug.

You don't know how good that hug felt! For a lonely kid, a long way from home, living in a dorm full of guys, that hug felt wonderful! "You must be one of those Air Force guys!" she said. At that point, the last thing I wanted to be was "one of those Air Force guys." "We have a whole row of you guys," she said, and actually took me by the hand and led me up to the second row. There were a bunch of people I recognized from my dorm! They were guys I hadn't met but had seen in the kitchen, laundry room, or at work. I had no idea there were so many Christians around me!

With all its weaknesses, this is the beauty of the church. It brings all different kinds of people together. People who normally wouldn't ever know each other build relationships because they **want** to, not because they **have** to. It's not like work or extended family where you **have** to be in relationship. Church is a place where you purposely go to build relationship, and, man, it is a challenge sometimes to build relationship with people who are so different! **But**, that is also the point.

Maturity is going from "it's all about me" to "it's not about me at all." Most people will never make this transition. They will live their whole lives thinking only about how every situation or circumstance will affect **them**. They will consume 99% of their resources on themselves. Worse, some will abuse credit and eat up 120% or even 150% of their income. They have no time to give and no available resources to be generous, but just consume everything that is even close to them—finances, relationships, resources, time—all consumed without a second thought.

God is aggressive about getting us where we are interested in something bigger than ourselves.

One thing I have learned on this journey is that God is aggressive about getting us to the place where we are interested in something bigger than ourselves. When I stepped into this church, I didn't know I had just stepped into this process!

The concert was just ok, but the atmosphere was awesome! They opened with worship. Now, I was used to only an organ and piano. My mom could play a mean organ with the pedals and all! They had a full band—drums, bass guitar, electric guitar, and even some brass! Wow, from the moment they started, I got goose bumps. The songs weren't hymns but were personal songs of worship. They spoke to me. They spoke to where I was. I spoke through the songs to God. I could **feel** the presence of the Holy Spirit! This was awesome! The church had about 250 people at that time, and the amazing thing was **everybody** was worshipping, **participating**. They actually looked … happy … in church!

I never went anywhere else. I never missed a service. I would work all night, take my lunch, and come to service and sleep through the sermon. In the churches I grew up in, no doubt, someone would have seriously reprimanded me; but the pastor of Great Falls Christian Center, Bob Johnson, with grace in his heart, understood I had worked all night. He simply told me, "Someday you will reap the fruit of being faithful to the house of the Lord," and, man, did I ever!

Pastor Bob had come from Alaska in the late seventies and started Great Falls Christian Center. He stood over six feet tall and had a deep passion for the people of God in the city of Great Falls. Part of that passion was to raise-up young leaders.

As awesome as this was going, there was still the issue of my not liking the church. My heart was broken. That hadn't changed. I was happy to be there to get what I needed from God, but I certainly wasn't going to enter into any relationships. I would slip in, sit in the back row, and slip back out when Pastor Bob prayed at the end of his message. I did this for a while. One Sunday, as usual, Pastor Bob started his end-of-message-prayer, and I turned to slip out. There standing in the doorway, was Lee Barrows, my future father-in-law. "I've been waitin' for you boy," were his exact words. A short, stocky farm boy with huge fingers and a heart as big as any you will ever see, he said he wanted to take me out for lunch. Man, I didn't know if I wanted this. This is not good, I thought; but I was lonely, and I longed to talk to someone who cared, so before I knew it, I said yes.

Now Pastor Lee is one of the nicest people I have ever met in my entire life. He is a big, jolly teddy bear, and he can really lower your defenses ... but mine were pretty high.

We ate great burgers at a smoky, dark, local diner named Eddie's Supper Club. He asked all the normal questions about my life, family, career, and such.

But then he asked, "What does God have for you? What's in you?"

Honestly these were not questions I had asked myself. I knew what I **wanted** to do, but what does God have in **His** heart for me? I really didn't know how to process or answer that question. Does God really have something in **His** heart for me? I guess I knew the Scriptures, "For I know the plans I have for you … " and, "You were created in Christ Jesus to do good works that He prepared in advance for you to do."

But I had never really applied them to myself. Did I just blow it? Could God have really put me in this little city in the middle of nowhere? Or, did I go wrong somewhere and miss what God had? But when I was about to switch orders at basic training I **did** hear God's voice say, "That is not where I sent you." Now I was sitting here with a pastor asking me, "What does God have in **His** heart for you?"

QUESTIONS:

• Have you ever heard His voice of direction?

• Might God have you where you are to take you to a place He wants you to go?

• Where might that be?

• Do you have someone asking you the tough questions?

• What does God have in His heart for you?

I stayed pretty guarded throughout that lunch appointment, but Lee saw something in me and began to reach out to me every opportunity he had. Now, I don't know if you have gotten this yet, but God is more interested in your growth than in your comfort. He doesn't mind putting you in **really** uncomfortable situations if it will help you to grow. We hate it, but the end result is good. I was in electronics, and my job was to keep those big ICBM missiles on line 24/7. There was only one problem—they didn't break that often. I found myself working **5 days a month,** if I was lucky. I even remember months where I only went in for a half-day test and a half-day shop day. **Two half-days** in a month. I was bored out of my gourd.

God is more interested in your growth than in your comfort

What I didn't know was that God was sneaking up on me! I played racquetball three times a day. I ran. I hiked. I rode my bike … For a guy who has some form of ADD, just crawling by day after day was bad news. Most guys just laid around watching TV all day, got into trouble after they spent the night out drinking, and spent money like crazy because of the boredom. **Most** guys got so lazy when they **did** have to finally work, they had the audacity to **complain** about it! For me, it was miserable. Talk about not feeling productive!

Months passed, and, finally, Lee found out I had nothing to do and started sending people after me. "Will you help us with the lawn?" was the first request. At first, I was hesitant to help; I did all this as a PK, and it was never appreciated … just expected. But I was bored! So finally, I gave in. I mowed the grass … then it was spraying gasoline (I mean "Roundup®") on the weeds in the cracks in the parking lot. After that, it was taking down the old sanctuary lights so the new ones could be installed; then it was helping finish the walls and build the stage. Finally, it became, "Will you just keep regular hours so we know when you are coming in so we can leave a list for you?" Do you see where this is going?

As I served, something strange began to happen in me. I *fell in love* with the House of the Lord—not the people, but the place and the atmosphere. **This** is why at Church for Life we believe so strongly in serving. We actually ask people to not even attend our church if they don't intend to serve in some way. There are things accomplished by serving that can't be accomplished in any other way. Someone who comes unwilling to serve will just eat up precious seats and resources and want to be pampered and personally pastored. People who start serving will begin to self-lead, grow and heal—all part of their own process God is working within them. The **best** way we have found to get people to grow is to get people to serve.

So now, within just a couple months of serving at Great Falls Christian Center, I now had regular set hours to come in, grab my list, and go to work. I began to love what God was doing in me as I contributed to the King and His Kingdom. As much time as I was spending around there, people were beginning to notice me and see potential in me. They were beginning to think of bigger things for me. Because my heart was still so dark, this was getting to be a problem. I honestly did not want to even be around church people.

One night though, we were worshipping, and a guy down from me in the row began speaking in tongues quietly between songs! I froze, thinking *This is not one of **those** churches is it?* I couldn't believe it. I went home and called my dad, and he said, "Run, Rob; run! They will shove that stuff down your throat. Get out of there!" But I couldn't. I loved the presence of the Holy Spirit that I could feel especially during worship. I had never before been in a Spirit-filled atmosphere. I just decided I would put up my guard and not let anyone "push" that stuff on me. The poor first guy who did talk to me got rebuffed and an earful. I am sure he left saying, "What just happened there?" The word got out, and they pretty much left me alone on that subject after that. But God wouldn't, and it would come up again later at the most inopportune moment.

Here's the deal. I loved God, loved serving Him by serving in the house of the Lord, but when it came to His people ... that was where I drew the line. I *still* hated church people. Growing up, my brothers, my dad, and I had a quartet, and we sang together at different places. I had been singing since Mom would stand my brother Ken and I on the piano bench on either side of her, and we would sing parts while she sang the lead to make a trio. People soon noticed I could sing, and they asked me to be on the worship team. Again, I was reluctant, but really this wasn't working with people. I could show up and do my thing and leave, still keeping a bit of distance.

One Sunday as I was sitting there, this girl I had never seen walked from the back all the way to the front straight to the piano and began to play for worship. She was absolutely phenomenal! She was beautiful, a worshipper, and as I found out, Pastor Lee's daughter, home from Portland Bible College. I was mesmerized.

Unfortunately, all the other guys were too! In that Air Force town, there was probably a 10 to 1 ratio of guys to girls. In the church, it was even worse. Poor Cindy and her sister Abby were two of just a few pretty, eligible girls there, and **all** the guys had "words from God" about marrying them. One thing both of them were pretty clear about is that they would **never** marry a "jetter," the local term for an Air Force guy. Well, that left **me** out, so I didn't really try. We did begin to hang out though at different functions. By this time, they had talked me into leading worship, and after losing a youth leader and many failed attempts at finding another one, they asked me to help with the youth. I didn't even like kids! What was I doing here?

> *It all happened so quietly,*
> *I barely noticed what was going on in my*
> *heart.*

The only other option I had was lying around all day in the dorm with a bunch of drunks. One in particular was a guy named Sean. He was really nice when he was buzzed. "How you doing, man?" he would always ask when I ran into him. Somehow he ended up at church, got saved and began to grow. He and Abby now live in California and are pastors with us! I finally found out he liked Abby and admitted I liked Cindy. Sean and I had an instant bond. Another one of the drunks in the dorm was a rugby player nicknamed "Duke." He ended up in church also and eventually he and his wife became our assistant youth pastors for over eight years! They also now live in California and are pastoring with us too! So here I am in the Air Force, with the government's paying my paycheck, but now I had regular hours at the church doing worship, youth, and building maintenance … and I didn't even like church people! It all happened so quietly, I barely noticed what was going on in my heart.

QUESTIONS:

• How has God used difficult circumstances to soften your heart?

• How have you experienced a God who is more concerned with your growth than your comfort?

chapter
the woman i needed

Cindy had introduced me to a friend who lived in Tacoma, Washington, and we had started long-distance dating. One day, she shared with me her dream was a farm with horses; I knew there was no future for us. Me on a farm—was not going to happen. I am a city guy. After I broke up with her, Cindy and I had coffee. She wanted to make sure that "I was ok." After some conversation, she asked why we had broken up, and I just simply told her I was looking for a girl similar to her. I had seen in her things I realized I wanted in my future wife—a worshipper who was strong, yet possessing tons of grace, very determined, and not needy.

To my surprise, she responded saying she admired me too, and I had a lot of qualities she had written down when she was a girl. She had a list! This *list* even had dark hair. She was a very intense, intentional girl. We decided to start dating that night.

As we started dating, we were having an absolute blast. One night after serving together, we were laughing and having fun when she shocked me. "You know I would never marry a guy who wasn't baptized in the Holy Spirit with speaking in tongues and the manifestation of the gifts of the Spirit. He just wouldn't be able to lead me like I will need to be led." Well *that* went over like a lead balloon and put a damper on the night! We talked for a bit, then I went home.

I didn't believe in "all that supernatural, goofy stuff!" We had been taught all of this stuff was sensationalism, and the tongues thing was of the Devil! I wouldn't do it for a girl; that's for sure! So I started searching the Scriptures, and I got a simple book from Jack Hayford entitled, *Baptism with the Holy Spirit*. As I began to read, I realized there were a lot of Scriptures we never talked about growing up. We never preached them or even addressed them. We avoided them. So I called up my dad, asking, "What about **this** scripture?"

"Well Son, we don't understand that, so we just don't go there."

"What? How about this one," I tried again.

"Well, we don't understand that, so we don't go there either. We believe that it may just have been something poured out on the disciples and not for today," he concluded.

Man, that didn't work for me. I saw a passion in Spirit-filled people, and I wanted it. So I began to read every Holy Spirit scripture and asked for an outpouring and complete baptism of the person of the Holy Spirit. I went up for prayer for it several times. People would gather around me and start praying in the Spirit really loudly. That didn't do a thing for me. Actually, it made me mad every time. I just wanted to crawl out between their legs and disappear. I wonder if they would have even noticed that I was gone!

Finally, one day at a Sunday morning service, one of the elders had a word of knowledge that I was going through something God wanted to solve today. As I told him about this struggle with the control issue of my tongue, he said, "Man, you love to sing; I would wait until everybody leaves and just go up front and sing and worship until God pours out His Spirit on you." So that's what I did.

Everyone left, and I went up front; the moment I opened my mouth to sing, unknown words I had never spoken came out. A new mainline opened up between my spirit and God's spirit, and I have never been the same. I changed so drastically that my family, who up until that point thought I had lost my salvation when I chose a different kind of church than the ones they approved of, began to be interested in what was going on in my heart. I began to mentor my little brother and my older brother, both who now are filled with the Spirit and serve with us today. God has even given me many opportunities to mentor my own parents.

So now I was baptized in the Holy Spirit, but Cindy broke up with me. Can you believe that? Her heart just changed. She gave me the "I love you like a brother" thing, which is the ultimate dis! For the next eight months, I had to go back to God and figure out what He was trying to do in me. I got a lot of advice and talked with a lot of people, but no one could understand how her heart could just "shut off" like that. Over those months, we talked several times, and she would say there was just "nothing there." She would even apologize! We continued to do ministry together, worship, youth, and nursing home, among other things, and I never gave up on what I was feeling inside, although I almost did. Close friends were telling me to "move on." I would go over to the church late at night and play lonely tunes on my saxophone. I was hurting … again.

God began to peek through all of that and show me I was rather possessive of everything He gave to me—like He wasn't good enough to me, like I didn't trust Him to bring me something good, and then keep it good. This made me "own" it and get controlling about it. It wasn't very obvious; I was able to hide it pretty well, but it was there. Those toxins I still had from seeing my dad hurt, from seeing churches ripped out from his hands, from seeing old ladies give our family an up or down vote changing our lives, were still making their presences known. When I had something, I was going to be in control if it.

When I had something, I was going to be in control if it.

But now, I had the power of the Holy Spirit. He was all over me, speaking to me words of knowledge about myself and my situation. I could feel God working in me. Then a guy who Cindy had met at a wedding was "driving through" and wanted to spend the weekend seeing her and the church. This was the ultimate test—ultimate surrender. Cindy asked if I would hang out with them so it wouldn't be awkward—for whom? It was certainly awkward for me! I hated this guy, and I had never even met him; but I had a decision to make. I could live in the default of insecurity, or live in the power of this new access I had to the Holy Spirit. So I decided to just be there for her. He rolled in and we hung out all weekend. He was a singer, and we **even did a special song** on Sunday all together! It was a weird weekend, but it was an amazing opportunity to try out this new supernatural power I had access to! It worked, but Cindy withdrew again after that. After this, I had space to check my heart yet again when God told me why He had taken her heart away from me; He told me, "She is my daughter before she is your wife, and don't ever forget that."

Weeks after that revelation, we were dating again; five months later, we were married. The last 15 years have been the best of my life. I married the most incredible woman, who was not only exactly what I **wanted**, but she was also what I **needed**! She is honest with me, yet so honoring. She gives me boundaries, yet total respect. She is a ball of fire, yet full of grace. But I never forget who owns her heart. Before she was my wife, she was God's daughter. Thank you, Holy Spirit!

QUESTIONS

• What do you believe about the Holy Spirit?

• How are you experiencing the power of the Holy Spirit in your life?

• When is the last time you pushed through one of your own opinion barriers?

• How do you see the people in your life? As people to hold onto or as God's sons and daughters?

chapter

PK invitation to destiny

Things started happening fast. I didn't even feel like I was in the military. I hardly ever put my uniform on, but I was on-call all the time, so I never knew when I would have to go out to a missile site within an hour.

Other than that, the military was just God's way of getting me to Nineveh—I mean Great Falls—and providing a paycheck while I came into ministry at the church.

Cindy and I had started doing youth with about eight kids whose parents *made* them come. They didn't want to be there, and frankly we didn't want them there either. I remember begging a mom, "Please don't make him come if he doesn't want to!" We stuck in there though and ended up with some of the greatest kids and the largest youth ministry in our city.

Finally, it happened. Pastor Bob called me in and told me I had a "five-fold gifting." A five-fold what? I had never heard of that. We never talked about this stuff growing up. What he meant in simple language was I was probably called to be in some type of ministry. I had one of the five-fold (apostle/prophet/pastor/evangelist/teacher) giftings to give to the Body of Christ. As he explained this, a darkness began to creep over my heart, like the fog that rolls in every night here on California's central coast. You can watch it literally roll in and feel it as it … whoosh … envelops you in a damp chill.

As Bob was talking, my heart was screaming, "NO, God, this isn't fair. You **know** how hurt I've been by ministry. You **know** how I despise the thought of spending my life for people who will never appreciate it with no promise of a secure salary, retirement, or career. I don't mind serving You 'on the side,' but I won't pastor." I left that meeting with all kinds of flight thoughts going through my head. Maybe I would just retire from the military, and **then** I could serve God on the side **after** my career. As I talked to my parents, they agreed. Get secure **first**, and **then** do ministry, because you never know when it will fail you. Ministry is a big unknown. I cooled off big time to the idea.

But God didn't. He just kept on with the plan, giving us success in youth ministry. Kids were getting saved, and we were in all the schools through clubs, preaching, and worshipping. In one school, the club had to meet in the hallway; we would set up a whole band in the public high school hallway, and our youth band would play as kids from all other kinds of churches gathered around to worship. It was amazing. That keyboardist in our youth band would eventually marry my younger brother, be a missionary to war-torn Kosovo, and then end up here with us in California helping run our small groups, and, yes, still playing keyboard and leading worship.

Cindy and I had bought a little 708 square-foot house. It was **tiny**, but cute, and we had what we called the "Saturday night hang" there every week, as well as Wednesday night youth. More than 30 kids would come over, literally invading our house, breaking things, hanging out on our roof, falling **off** our roof, and eating us out of house and home. This is when I got my first ministry budget: $25 a month to help keep groceries on our shelves! With a youth ministry involving 200-300 kids over 10 years, we were able to see a lot of patterns.

Over those years we saw thousands of kids come through our youth ministry called Generation Church. As we watched, some went to Bible school and found great jobs and churches. We did lots of weddings as young people found part of their destinies in finding their spouses. We also saw tragedy. Kids went off to college and entered the drug scene, alcoholism, divorce, and unwed pregnancies. Many kids went off into the world and were talked right out of their faith and consider themselves agnostics today. Kids would come home hard, looking like they had been to war. Some of our kids are in prison today. Others are married to unsaved spouses. They are living miserable lives in the default. We finally began to realize and teach the common denominator to the kids who were doing well and thriving. It was simply this: Kids who did well had found a local church—a group of believers! They had **surrounded** themselves with believers. This would begin to change the way I looked at the church.

Finally, Pastor Bob asked me if I would get out of the military and come on staff as an administrator/youth guy. Against my inner screams and my parents' judgment, I did just that. Cindy and I were now on staff at a church, and, believe it or not, I was cool with that because I was **just** serving and administrating. We were making $900 a month at the church, less than half of what I made in the military, so I worked part-time, as did Cindy, to make up for what we needed to live. I drove long hours in a company truck as a promotional director for a local business to 76 insurance agents every month. I wrote many youth messages out on those desolate Montana roads with the steering wheel in one hand and a pen in the other.

But even in that job, God was training me for the future when we would plant a church in a place we had never been, a place where we knew no one, a "foreign country" I had never been to called California. In our city even today, we are known for our unique promotions. We have even helped other churches in this area.

God has placed our destiny just beyond our reach, and it is on purpose.

I learned not to despise the classroom of loneliness, the classroom of pressure, the classroom of boredom, the classroom of confrontation and offense, and what I think is God's favorite: the classroom of situations bigger than I am.

Like Noah, Daniel, Gideon, David, Joseph, Paul, and many others in the Bible, God has placed our destiny just beyond our reach, and it is on purpose. Our destiny can only be found by accessing a power beyond our own to reach it—the power of the Holy Spirit. This is called faith. It's only "by faith" that we have Hebrews 11, the hall of honor for the great people in the Bible. All they did was access a power beyond their own in order to walk in faith. Don't despise God's strategic classrooms.

QUESTIONS:

• What are you doing right now that seems challenging, or even out of the ballpark?

• Could your present circumstances be training for what is in God's heart for you?

• How can doing your absolute best right now prepare you for destiny?

In the middle of all this doing, something was about to blow up in my face. Something I didn't even know was still there. Something I wouldn't have expected would come out of me. I *felt* pretty healthy, but I wasn't. The elders decided they would like to ordain me. What was the big deal? I was already *doing* the stuff of a pastor; I was even *acting* like one. Most people were even calling me a youth pastor.

But this rocked my world. My mind went crazy with thoughts of being taken advantage of and of what it would mean to be a pastor. Simply put, being a pastor is helping people carry the worst, heaviest, most dysfunctional burdens. I have heard the most hideous stories in my office. People have laid out their stories of survival in a fallen world. I knew what this was. I had seen it, felt it, and lived it. I had heard the late night conversations; I grew up hearing people crying out in our living room. I remembered when people would stop by at all hours to just "dump." I knew this life. Most people look at a pastor and judge what they do by the 40 minutes they see him preach on Sunday. I love to preach; this job would be cake if that were all I had to do. It's the *other* 60-90 hours with all the people that are what a pastor *really* does. However, what really struck fear into my heart was I knew if I did this—if let myself become a pastor—I would fail like my dad did. I saw his life crumble and fall apart. I saw him fail, and when I was a child, I decided deep in my heart I would never put myself in that position. NO, this was not the life for me.

Meanwhile, I was preaching, leading worship, leading kids to the Lord, and raising up an awesome group of 30 adult leaders for Generation Church. We were doing summer camps and winter camps, where kids' lives were being radically altered. This was an **inner** battle. This was among me, God, and the Devil himself—and I was getting worked over. As the time grew closer to when they wanted to ordain me, I started growing frantic and a bit angry inside. "Why me, God?" I would plead. "I've already had enough of this! Pick someone who **wants** to do this. There are plenty out there. I **don't** want to do this, and You know that. This is so cruel of You! I told You since I was a kid that I wouldn't do this. Father, would You just take this cup. … "

Not too long after that, I was leading worship at our men's retreat in Lincoln, Montana, where I told God, "We are going to duke this out up here, gloves off. And whatever I come away with—yes or no— we will never have this conversation again." I was serious. At the retreat center, I set everything up, led worship, and did my thing; but in private, I was wrestling. During breaks, I would take walks on the road that had been chiseled out of the 12 feet of snow, all the while wrestling with God.

I felt like Jacob the night he fought all night with God. I fought too, fighting and scratching; my reasons didn't even have to be fair or Scripture-based. This was the last demonic lie of fear inside me, and it wasn't going to go away easily. No one even knew I was in the battle for my very life and destiny. Throughout the weekend, I did ministry when things were in session and privately battled when we had breaks and prayer times, but especially at night. That is when God spoke to me. He actually made me a deal.

Keep your integrity, and keep your heart soft.

He told me, "If you will do just two things: **1) Keep your integrity, and 2) keep your heart soft.** If you will do these two things, I will do the rest. I will build a church that even the gates of hell won't be able to conquer. I will see to your success, if you will see to your heart and integrity."

"Wow! That's a simple plan!" I thought. "I can do that!"

A few months later we had a powerful ordination service and I was set-in as a pastor.

God builds the church and ministry. Man, He does an incredible job! The Bible says when the church is built this way, all of our hard work won't ever be a waste (Psalm 127:1); I came home with a new plan. I was going to guard my heart and let God build whatever He wanted to. I would let **Him** bring the success. I found great peace in this and still do. As I relinquished control of things, God took over and made them grow! In fact, the more I step back these days, the better things seem to grow. The more I try and control them, the smaller and less healthy they are. Now, I don't worry about failing like my dad did.

Today, I live by those two things. I keep careful watch over my heart and integrity. Cynicism and negativity are what defeated my dad.

Every day, I consider the health of my heart and life. I have mentors all around me. I see two different counselors and a whole boatload of local pastors I relate to. I have met with a small group of pastors weekly for the last five years and am now the president of the ministerial association with around 90 pastors involved.

I take relationships very seriously in regards to my health. Cindy and I work hard to see that our marriage is fun and fresh. One of the first things I look for in any leader is a happy, healthy spouse! She is my wife—my confidant—and we are working hard on raising healthy, happy, and growing kids.

QUESTIONS:

- How have you been wrestling with God?

- What does He wants for Your life? Will You submit to His desire for your life?

There was a day I almost quit. It was after the ordination, in the middle of success in youth ministry, with other youth pastors' looking to us and senior pastors' sending their youth pastors to us. In the middle of *tons* of fruit, I almost quit. My son Andrew had been born a bit more than a year before, and we were pregnant again. We were excited—maybe a girl this time? We were planning, getting the baby's room ready when we went in for our second ultrasound. They even let us bring a video tape so we could watch it in the future. It was an exciting time.

We went into the little dark room, and the nurse put the jelly on the belly and started looking with the wand. We had done this before with Andrew, so we knew what to look for. You look for form, shape, and most importantly, the heartbeat. As she looked and looked, she got quiet and went to get the doctor. He came in and looked for himself, then just turned to us and matter-of-factly said, "Folks, your baby is dead."

Cindy began to cry and fell over into my arms; I began to cry, and the doctor left to give us some time. What do you say? What *can* you say? A dream had died.

Something in me died too. That darkness of being taken advantage of began to roll in. "God, I'm taking care of hundreds of other people's kids, doing lock-ins, staying up all night, breaking up beer parties when parents are on vacation ... **and You kill my baby**? If that is how You are going to treat me, I'm not working for You. I will honor You and live for You, but I'm not going to preach for You. I'm done. Find someone else."

That was the day I almost quit, and all we have realized over the last ten years would have been lost. The hundreds we now call friends, elders, pastors, apprentices, and new believers would have never happened.

Don't despise the classroom of loss and pain

Now, I want to tell you why I not only love my wife, but also have the utmost respect for her. One day she got a revelation. She said, "You know what, babe? This is going to make us better pastors. This will help us to relate to people going through great loss over the years. We can let this make us better!" With that, her countenance changed; her attitude changed. She stepped back into faith. She still remembers May 15 every year, the day we lost our little baby, but she has used our loss and pain to grow. We have since had opportunities to relate to many people experiencing loss: the parents who lost their 16-year-old when she was hit by a drunk driver; the suicides and suicide attempts; a woman, our friend, hanging from the basement rafter; and the funeral I did not too long ago for a 4-month-old baby. However, most significantly, we could relate to the recent death of our own youth pastor's son. With a guitar in my hand, we worshipped as the doctors began pulling the plugs to his life suport.

Don't despise the classroom of loss and pain. Yes, it was tough to reconcile that. I just had to put my trust back in the Father. Someday, I will meet my baby in heaven, and someday, I might see the clearer purpose. But, for now, I totally trust my King. I came too close that day to throwing in the towel. PK, don't quit. You don't know what you and thousands of others might miss. I wouldn't trade what we have now for anything.

Job said, "Should we accept only good things from the hand of God and never anything bad?" Job 2:10 (NLT)

Is that not just so stinking selfish? But we do. We have created this theology of all good from God and, in turn, created a generation of Christians who will quit serving God the first time He doesn't do something they think He should have. I almost joined their ranks. Where would I be today? What would I have missed out on? I think about that group of teens and college kids flooding the front for worship every Wednesday night at Generation Church—kids I love *so much*; it brings tears to my eyes that I might have missed being a part of their lives. Again, I beg you. PK, don't quit.

QUESTIONS:

• Have you ever quit or felt like quitting? What did you do? What was the outcome?

• Do you have people to support/surround you when the pain strikes?

• What hard times have made you stronger/better because of them?

1980

me

me

5 + 3½

1995

me

The incredible fam!

As hard as it was to lose our baby, there were many other hard things to come. It's right here, at this point in this book, that I must address a subject I am so passionate about that I talk about it very often. It's today that this principle is more real to me than ever. It's the subject of self-leadership. You see, for many of us, when we think of leadership ... we always think of those *we* lead.

That is a leader, but not necessarily a *good* leader. I know you've probably heard this or a variation on it a million times, because it's been around forever: a good leader is a 360-degree leader! Imagine a compass—north, south, east, and west. Almost every time the word leadership is mentioned, in what direction do people generally think? South. It's just how we've been taught to think as PKs.

But many people don't realize you need to have leadership flowing in all four directions—north, south, east and west.

NORTH - Every good leader should have relationships above where they are.
SOUTH - You aren't a leader if no one is following.

EAST - Those who are around you, such peer relationships, family, and friends.

WEST - Other teams, ministries, departments, and collaborations, creating win-win situations.

This is a well-rounded leader; but there is one direction left! Perhaps the most overlooked leadership challenge is the one in the middle. By far, your toughest leadership challenge will be leading yourself. See, **this** is why great leaders fall.

Self-leadership is truly tested during our times of crises. In that last chapter, I shared the loss of our baby. Now, let me bring you to the present and what I faced today.

I got up early this morning and headed for the church about 7 a.m. On my way, a guy stepped out in front of me right off the sidewalk, and I hit him. I knelt with him in the middle of the street as he lay dying, waiting for help to arrive. He didn't make it.

Now, I sit here several hours later, replaying and replaying it in my mind over and over to see if there was something I could have done differently. He just never saw me and stepped right in front of me the moment I came by. His head went completely through my windshield, a picture I will have in my mind forever. But now I sit here. It's Saturday. I have a word in my heart for my church tomorrow—a three-week series that I have been planning. The subject?

Self-leadership.

My wife is in Montana playing at a wedding today. She has no idea this tragedy has happened. The kids are downstairs. My team has come and prayed for me; offers are coming in from other pastors to guest speak for me tomorrow. But I am here, ready to take on the challenge of self-leading. Just two hours ago, I was kneeling in the street with a dying man I had hit. For sure, this effects how I feel; but does that really effect **who** I am? I feel miserable, horrible. I just went to the hospital to see if I could pray with the family; there was none there. Frankly, I am traumatized and have whiplash. **But**—this is a time when there are no words people can say to help me. This is a time when I want my wife to be here, but she's not. This is a time when I want to know the outcome of the process (Will I get sued? How long will my car be impounded? Was I speeding?) … but I can't.

> *The only thing I can do is step from the natural into the supernatural.*

The only thing I can do is reach down deep inside to my spirit and step from the natural into the supernatural. I'm going to preach tomorrow. I am going to listen to worship music all evening and be on the front row worshipping in the morning. Actually, **leading** in worship from the front row is how I think about it. How is this possible? Self-leadership. The principle of self-leadership will see you through to the next level.

Watch this … David had just fought an awesome battle and was coming home pumped!

> *Three days later, when David and his men arrived home at their town of Ziklag, they found that the Amalekites had made a raid into the Negev and had burned Ziklag to the ground. [2] They had carried off the women and children*

and everyone else but without killing anyone. ³ When David and his men saw the ruins and realized what had happened to their families, ⁴ they wept until they could weep no more. ⁵ David's wives ... were among those captured. ⁶ David was now in serious trouble because his men were very bitter about losing their wives and children, and they began to talk of stoning him.

1 Samuel 30:1-6 (NLT)

Now this is a tough place to be in ... no one is with David, not even his wife! God will make sure that at some point we get to this place of discovery!

You see it over and over again in the Bible—Noah and the Ark; Gideon and the idols; Moses over and over again; Daniel in the lion's den; Shadrack and Nebuchadnezzer's golden statue; Peter and the gentiles; John on the island of Patmos.

What we are discovering is not what's in our pastor, our spouse, our church, our boss, or our job; what we really discover is what is in **us**!

So ... David had to mobilize his troops ... so where did he start? Did he go north to his mentors, south to his mighty men, east to his brothers, or west to another king? No! 1 Samuel 30:6 (NKJV™) tells us, "But David strengthened himself in the Lord his God."

David went straight to God to strengthen **himself.** He was his own starting point. David understood the importance of self-leadership. Most people think they can lead other people ... but can you lead yourself? Although it's not talked about a lot, it's probably the most important spot in the compass. If the middle is off, everything is off, and the needle just rattles around.

In the same way, if your self-leadership is off, you will look around and interpret everyone within sight as being "off." This leads to frustration and disillusionment with people. What you have to do is put the responsibility for spiritual growth back into your own hands.

If you can't, then you are only as strong as the time and energy your pastor, friends, spouse, girlfriend or boyfriend can give you! God forbid at some point in your life they aren't there. It is impossible for the church in one and a half hours a week to give you all you need to grow into a mature, God-focused, people-oriented Christian and leader. What we as pastors are seeing is that as much as we *want* to do it for you, it's still a personal relationship with Jesus that makes you grow! Duh!

Today, tragedy struck my life, and here is where I am leading myself—right to Jesus. *He* will see me through this. *His* Spirit will bring me comfort, and I will grow. PK, if you are going to get through this struggle, as well as many that will come, you are going to have to be able to reach way down deep inside and *lead yourself* back to Jesus!

QUESTIONS

- What is the last crisis you faced? How did you respond?

- Have you ever had a moment in your life when everything changed?

- What does self-leadership look like to you?

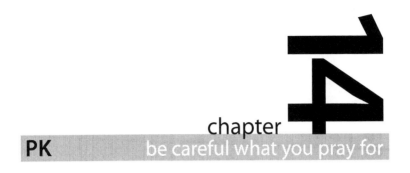

As I write this, a couple of weeks have passed since the horrible accident I described in the last chapter; and yes, I'm okay. I have gathered every great friend I have around me and gone to Jesus almost minute by minute at times. I am sleeping again, and God has broken that spirit of mourning and replaced it with my regular spirit of joy! I have learned two things from this tragedy. The first is if you have enough good people around you, it's almost hard **not** to be healthy. The second is that the Word of God simply works. You can trust it. Everything I have preached all these years worked for me through one of the toughest crises I have ever faced. Of course, the opposite can also be true.

Be careful what you pray for.

Several years ago, while we were still in Montana, we picked up this little book called *The Prayer of Jabez*, by Bruce Wilkinson. 1 Chronicles 4:10 *"Oh, that You would bless me indeed, and enlarge my territory, that Your hand would be with me, and that You would keep me from evil, that I may not cause pain!" (NKJV™)*

Four little harmless things to pray … right? We started to pray this as a family, not realizing God actually hears and answers our prayers. It is amazing—and the default—that we pray and don't expect it to actually happen.

I soon after found myself on a mission trip to Shanghai, China, with 80 kids. It was technically a "cross-cultural exchange," but it was our goal to share the gospel if they asked. Man, did they ask! For almost a month, we hung out, went to their homes and shared 16 hours a day with about 300 teens from China. I had 20 Chinese teens in my class and three American teen "mentors." We had a blast.

A few weeks after I got back from this life-changing experience in China, I received an e-mail from the principal of the school. He was general secretary of his branch of the communist government, inviting us to come live on the campus in China and teach English. They would pay us well, send our son to an international school, and we would have a car with a driver! I told them part of our culture was having a church. They agreed to give me the nice space we had met previously in for our team meetings to have church every Sunday!

"Don't ever laugh off an opportunity God gives you."

I couldn't believe it; actually … I laughed it off. With all we were doing and involved in around our city, there was no way we could go do this. I showed it to my pastor, and he said, "Don't ever laugh off an opportunity God gives you. Go talk to the elders." So one by one, I sat down with the elders and shared the opportunity; each one got excited and said they thought we should go!

Overwhelmed and at the same time eager to move in this new direction, we started to transition Generation Church. We already had our house for sale hoping to buy something much bigger, but that hadn't worked out. We realized that we had never been gone for more than three Wednesdays a year, but that year I had been gone 14! God was preparing us for this! We began to get excited, until one day, the China door slammed shut. Due to circumstances beyond our control, we weren't going. It was over.

I was stunned and shaken. I went back to the elders, and we all agreed the move to China just felt right. We waited. A couple of weeks later, our Pastor called us in and just said, "Let's plant a church!" The thought literally had never crossed our minds. Everyone knew we would just take Great Falls Christian Center someday for the current pastors; that was a given in our minds. Leave? Go? After all the investment? Where?

Pastor Bob told us to pick a place we might be interested in; he said he had a place in mind. Of course, we picked something cool and doable—Westerville, Ohio, right outside of Columbus. It was a growing, hip part of the city of planned communities where everyone drove a Land Rover or at least something cool! Houses were cheap, and jobs were plentiful. But Bob had another city in mind: Santa Maria, California.

We had often heard of this city from our Air Force friends. It also had a missile base like Great Falls, so we had a lot of people moving back and forth. Apparently, our pastor had considered this for a long time. I had never been to California, so I pictured the whole state to be like Compton and envisioned myself "packing heat" everywhere I went.

They decided to let us do a two-week scouting trip with no strings attached. Unfortunately, we flew into San Francisco instead of Los Angeles, because the drive down from San Francisco is **ugly**! Dry and brown, it kind of looked like parts of Montana. We weren't impressed.

For us, the traffic on the US Highway 101 was like driving the Indi 500. We stopped at a Marie Callender's and had one of the worst meals of our lives. Later, we stopped at a rest area, and Cindy came out of the bathroom white as a sheet. On the walls in permanent marker was a scene depicting a rape taking place. This was not going well. Further towards Santa Maria, we got to this strange grove of eucalyptus trees. When I went through them, I got an eerie feeling like I was going into Robin Hood's spooky Sherwood Forest.

The saving grace for Great Falls was the beautiful Missouri river. Movies have been made on that river. Celebrities used to come pay big bucks to raft down it. It flowed right behind our church. Well, Santa Maria had a "river" right on the north end of the city—at least it was blue on the map! Cool! As we approached the bridge on the 101, I even saw the sign that said "Santa Maria River." It was already dark, so I told everyone to look out to see the water, and, boy, were we disappointed! It was sand and weeds as far as the eye could see—just a big, dry riverbed. This was to be just the first of many disappointments in the next two weeks. When we got to our exit, the next thing I noticed were these bright, ugly, orange street lights. Everywhere else I had been, lights were always white; but these were "earth-friendly" lights. They were **horrible** is what they were! Even today, we have one right out in front of our house, and when I kiss the kids at night, their faces glow orange. If I am ever the mayor, I will try and change that!

We stayed with some friends and began our search of the city and for God's voice in this decision. I put 300 miles on our rental *just* in Santa Maria. I drove up and down every street I could find, waiting for a word from God. Day after day, we saw junked houses for $420,000; tiny, dirty condos for $290,000. Our current mortgage was $51,000 with a monthly house payment of $525 with taxes and insurance included. We actually bought our first house for $36,000 and had a payment of just $308 per month with taxes and insurance.

Here we were looking at half the house for $300,000! We were looking at a monthly payment of at least $2,000, if not more. We were overwhelmed! Plus, the city was not that great from what we could see. It was just a bunch of houses with no downtown. We didn't realize at the time how close to the beach and Santa Barbara we were! I drove and drove; my attitude's getting worse about it as the moments went by. It wasn't any better for Cindy. We weren't digging this place. The thing that drove me nuts was I just couldn't seem to hear anything from God! I had been asking for visions, angels to appear, signs in the heavens! Anything! I was desperate for a word from God.

I remember exactly where I was when he spoke. I was driving up over the Donovan bridge, not far from where we live today, when I hit the steering wheel and said, "God, why won't You just show me?" And He spoke …

QUESTIONS:

- Have you ever laughed off an opportunity God gave you?

• Have you ever had a open door close suddenly? How did you feel? What did you do?

• What "dangerous prayers" have you made? Have you asked for patience?

• What do you do when you just can't seem to hear from God?

• Can you actually direct your life by feeling bad or good "vibes"?

Let me take you back a few months to put this Word from God in context. Our small group had decided to do a spiritual gifts assessment. Everybody loves to hear about themselves, and there was an obvious buzz around the room while we were scoring. As I began to look at my score lines, I was pleased to see leadership way up at the top; prophetic was even high as well as a couple of others. So far, so good! But then my eyes drifted to see the score line drop to the dead bottom. I skipped a few to go over to see what in the world that would be. Faith. Yes, faith! I was dead bottom on faith!

Wait, we had a huge youth team, kids getting saved, we were in all the schools, doing city-wide stuff! This couldn't be correct, or all that stuff wouldn't be happening, right?

So I went up to the guys leading the group and said, "I don't believe this test. These are all questions about money, and yeah, I hate raising money; but I've got great faith!"

The leader just looked at me and said those dreaded words—"Yeah, well just pray about it."

So I did. God showed me I only stepped out when I had all my ducks in a row. After I had everything lined up and under control, then I was willing to do something. That was **not** faith. God then spoke to me that if I would let Him mess up my ducks, step out when nothing was lined up, and step out into a dark unknown … then through **real** faith, He would do more through me than I could ever imagine.

So I prayed that fateful prayer: **Lord, increase my faith!** Again, we don't expect God to answer, do we?

"God, why won't You just show me?"
"Because Rob, that wouldn't take faith."

So here I am, pounding the steering wheel, asking God, "God, why won't You just show me?"

He simply spoke to me, "Because Rob, that wouldn't take faith."

Man, I was stunned. I quietly drove back to where we were staying. When I came in the door, Cindy had also had conversation with God that she just had a bad attitude! Right then, we submitted to the Lord and decided we would just assume this was God; if it wasn't, then He could just slam the doors shut like He had with China.

After that moment, the divine appointments started to roll in. We went to look at a little condo, a dirty little place for around $300,000. When the realtor asked why we were moving to Santa Maria, I hesitated to say "In faith," so instead I said, "Well, we **may** be coming to start a church here." As soon as she heard that, she lit up and started telling us her husband had helped start a church. She grabbed her phone and dialed. Next thing I know, she handed me the phone. After a fairly awkward start, he told me he had helped start a local plant of The City Church. Well, we knew that name well! They were one of the main churches in our Ministers Fellowship International network: The City Church in Seattle. This church was 10 minutes away, and he invited us to come the next evening for their Wednesday night service.

The next night we walked into The City Church about five minutes before the service. We met the gentleman I had talked to on the phone, and he said, "Let's go meet our pastor."

No pastor wants to meet someone coming to start a "competing" church five minutes before getting up to preach. But he insisted, and down the hallway we went towards his office. After a knock on the door; it opened. There stood *a beautiful man!* How else could I say it? Now if you've never seen me, I am skinny, bald, and really white. This guy was tall, had a great tan, and *lots* of dark hair. He was just a beautiful man! His wife was gorgeous too! Right away, I wanted to get out of there. Insecurity set in instantly! He said, "Welcome!" and gave us a big hug. The service was starting, but he sat down with us and began to ask us about our intentions on planting in this area. He then asked me if I would have coffee with him the next morning.

Now, one thing the church planting books all say is when you move into a new area, all the pastors will give you the "stiff-arm of fellowship" because they don't know you or whether you want to help or hurt them. This is what I was expecting.

At coffee the next morning, we sat down to chat. After he had asked me quite a few questions, he looked at me and said, "Listen, God is about to do something here on the Central Coast; we *need* good, spirit-filled pastors and churches … *please* come.

We need you here." I was shocked. This wasn't how pastors were supposed to respond. I felt like this was God calling me here audibly for the first time—through another pastor! They ended up supporting us all the way through to our planting Sunday, praying for us all the way. Thank you, City Church in Nipomo and Pastors Rocky and Jean!

Well, that was encouraging, but we still had the issue of finding a house, job and all the details that would need to be in place to do this thing. But then **faith** is stepping out **before** all the details are in place … right?

So we went to one of the new housing developments that were sold out two years in advance and sat down with them. They had five houses left and were going to do the "lottery" system. They actually put names in a drum, turned it and pulled five names! The only problem is they only took a limited number of names; people would wait all night in line to be there in time to get their names in. You had to be there in person. Some friends of ours volunteered to go all night and get our names in for us; so **in faith**, we picked out our colors in about 15 minutes on our way out of town, and off we went back to our lives in Montana.

QUESTIONS:

- What are your strongest spiritual gifts?

- Where do you have the most room to grow? Are you willing to let God stretch you in this area?

- How has God messed up your ducks?

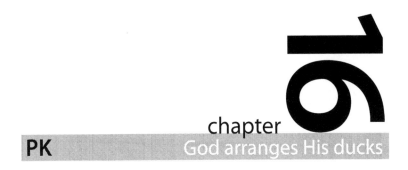

S o there I was, sitting back in my office in Montana thinking, "What was that? What just happened there?" We jumped back into our fast-paced life of youth ministry and tried to focus, but my mind was still spinning. I had just learned something about faith ... but would it work? "Just focus and get back to life," I told myself.

About two weeks later, I was at my desk when a call came through for me. I answered, and the voice said, "This is Theresa from River Oaks. You had applied for a house. Do you want one?"

"I think so," I said. She said she had thought about us and why were coming and decided if we wanted a house, she would make sure it happened. She offered to fax the remaining five lots and floor plans to us and we could just circle the one we wanted! As the fax machine began to buzz, I called Cindy frantically and asked her to get over to my office as soon as possible. In a matter of minutes, we were looking at the five remaining houses of a 500 house development. It's hard to tell what a house is like from black and white plans, so we circled the one with a curved driveway and the bigger back yard—our miracle house, where we live today, right beside that dry riverbed we passed on our way in. It's awesome for paintball, dirt bikes, hiking, and looking for wildlife.

Another miracle was getting financed for a house payment bigger than any monthly paycheck I had ever received! We needed a good fixed interest rate too. The most I had ever made monthly was about $2,200, and my new house payment was going to be close to $2500.

We had bought our first house in Montana with a monthly house payment of $308 **with** taxes and insurance. Our second had a monthly payment of $545, and now we were stepping into a payment of close to $2500! "Lord, increase my faith" is a dangerous prayer. *He might just answer you!* But to this day, we have never missed a payment.

So we did it. We announced to our church, to Generation Church, and our team that we were going to plant a church. People were happy, and people cried; but mostly what we wanted were people who would come with us. We had an incredible youth team of about 30 adults; some had been with us for over eight years, and some had even preceded us! Over the years, some of them had mentioned if we ever "got sent out," they would go in a heartbeat; so we anticipated having the support of a great team. We prayed for about 15 people to come with us to help us. Some drove to California to check it out, saw the huge prices and bad economy, and turned around to never even consider it again. Only Mandi, one shy college girl, said she had the faith to come with us if she could live with us. So she came. She faithfully ran our kids church for the first six years!

As we rumbled out of Great Falls, I realized this was the same point where I had first seen the city twelve years earlier at the beginning of my military duty. At that time, I was a bitter young man who was mad at the church and at church people for what they had done to destroy my dad … I had been determined to **love God** but not love His people.

Now, headed up and away from the Missouri River, my wife was crying gently beside me, leaving everything she had known, her home church, her family, the family farms, weddings, and get-togethers. I wondered what God had in store for us.

Andrew was in the middle playing Legos, not a care in the world. We had packed everything we owned into the biggest U-Haul available and had to give a bunch of stuff away that wouldn't fit. All of this for what? The Church? The Church who had so violently abused my family? My dad?

> *Only when you "lift up your eyes"*
> *will you ever be able to live as free and*
> *innocent.*

Well, not exactly. Let me give you a sneak peak at what you will read in the last chapters of this book. Here it is: brace yourself. If your eyes are focused on **people**, you will live your entire life bitter, angry and disappointed, trying to see life and yourself through angry comments, people's stares, and the rudeness and disrespect of this generation. Only when you "lift up your eyes" and focus on the Author and Finisher of your faith will you ever be able to live as free and innocent. It's not a pastor, parent, mentor, teacher or professor … or spouse. Oh, how we try to grab onto the next person to fulfill this role!

But none of these people will **finish** your faith. It's only Jesus.

In a 24 foot U-Haul, I left a great life, extended family, job, and a certain future … all for the King. I was no longer disappointed, because I was not looking to **people** to solve anything for me. I had "lifted up my eyes" and was no longer living in disappointment!

PK, if you are going to get through this, you are going to have to get your eyes off **people**. Until you get that one thing, you will live in disappointment every day.

More on that later.

QUESTIONS:

• How has God opened doors for you?

• When has God used strangers in your life?

• How have you been able to look beyond the hurts from your past?

When we arrived in Santa Maria, our house was still being built, so we lived with some friends until we got the keys. I had gotten a job selling cars and was now working 12-14 hour days, equaling 70+ hours a week; it was exhausting. The **worst** part was that they had promised me Sundays off, but when I showed up, they let me know **no one** got Sundays off. That was their highest selling day! So for three months, Cindy visited churches in town every Sunday while I worked those long hours. Talk about frustrating—I was here to plant a church! I would go out in between the Expeditions and cry out to God, "God, what are You doing! I am here to plant a church, and I can't even get the weekends off!" These were frustrating times, and the only support I had was $1,000 a month for one year from our sending church. This was not even half the house payment … I had to work hard to try and make it!

But the dealership was an incredible experience. It was probably the hardest job I have ever had. The hours were grueling, but that was just the start. I had to slam people into cars. We **had** to get the person on a test drive, or we could get fired. We just kind of kidnapped people by getting them in and driving off! I hated it … but I was learning a **lot!** The salesmen were the worst part. Generally, a car salesman has to be arrogant to handle the constant disrespect and rejection. As I stood out on "the point" where all the salesmen have to wait for someone to walk onto the lot, I endured the most vile stories of drug-filled orgies, drunken parties, and women, women, and more women. Some would not even make it home at night, so they would come from the bar back to the lot, sleep in their cars, wake up, and work another full day. This was **not** the place I wanted to be.

I complained to God, like Moses had, and like David had. But God simply said, "You pastor this flock that you don't want and I will give you the flock that you **do** want." It was as basic as that. ***Doing what is right in front of you with all of your heart*** is now how we define destiny at Church for Life, because that is what it took. So I started to pastor those guys. I started to listen to them, opened my heart to them, and gave some advice. The joke became that my office was the resident counseling center. Divorce, custody battles, depression, finances and budgeting— I did it all! I have now been a paid corporate chaplain for four years now at one of the largest corporations in our city. **All** of this experience was training for the thousands of appointments I have done there. God knows how to train us!

The worst guy of them all was an intimidating, tall, buff guy. He hated me. He made fun of me everyday. He was our top salesman, and he ruled the place. They gave him whatever he wanted. He threatened me almost daily with getting me fired. He could feel the pity I had for his drug-filled, crazy life. Making sometimes $20,000 a month, he lived on an air mattress on the floor of a one-room apartment, gambling, drinking, and spending every dime he made. As much money as he made, he was always broke. He would bum a dollar at a time from the guys to buy sodas. This was my opportunity. You see, he saw all of our paychecks, because he had access to the computers. He knew some months, I was only making $1500—not even enough to pay my house payment. He knew I had a lot of pressure on my moving, starting a church, and having a wife and kid. He **never** asked me, but every time he would ask to bum a dollar off the guys, I would offer him one. It drove him nuts!

One day, he snapped the dollar out of my hands and said, "What is **with** you?" I just kept giving him dollars. Eventually, I led him to the Lord. I led several of those guys to the Lord. But most importantly, I pastored the flock I **didn't** want, and God released me to the flock I did want. I had been there a few months when the general manager came to me one day and just said, "You can have Sundays off now."

I was shocked. I hadn't been doing any front work, sitting in coffee shops meeting people, or any of the other stuff the church planting books told me to do. I had just done what was right in front of me with all of my heart. For the last three months, Cindy and Andrew had been just visiting churches in the area to see what was out there. I called her and said, "We are starting church this Sunday!"

If we were going to do this, we needed to do it like we had done everything else—in faith.

She is so amazing and gracious. She and Mandi went out and hung hundreds of door hangers; we also put a little advertisement in the paper. All the church planting books at that time recommended starting out in your house with a small group and build from there. We felt like if we were going to do this, we needed to do it in faith.

We plunked down the $1,000 for a little hotel room across the 101 Highway and showed up that next Sunday ready to go. We set up all our stuff—projector, soundboard, keyboard, coffee, donuts—and we got ready to do church. The problem? We hadn't talked to **one person** who said they would come. I prepared the "team" and told them if we didn't have anyone we would just pray and keep on plugging away. Inside, I was a mess. We had left everything, come all this way, and endured all this—for what? Who knows? 10 a.m. came and no one appeared. 10:05 came and still no one came. I was getting physically sick to my stomach.

I told Cindy to keep an eye out for anyone to come, and I went to the other room we had rented for "kids church" and got on my face and said, "God, don't do this to me. Please don't humiliate me." As I was groveling on the floor before God, Cindy poked her head in and told me people were coming up the sidewalk! Little did I know how late Californians are to everything! Great man of faith that I was, I collected myself and walked out to greet the guests. We had 11 show up that day! I was giddy!

On the second week, we had a young, timid, stuttering college kid come in. His life was a mess. He grew up Buddhist, he had gotten his girlfriend pregnant, and they had just gotten married. He had no idea how to be a dad or a husband … but on his wedding day, right before he walked down the aisle, he had given his heart to Christ. We prayed with him and he told us his wife would never come to church. Her whole family was bitter from a family tragedy that had happened years ago. She had the baby that week so Cindy delivered some meals to her, and what do you know? She came to church that next Sunday and gave her heart to the Lord. Jeff and Cindy Hoyos have been our youth pastors now for six years and have touched the lives of literally thousands of kids in our city. We have one of the largest youth groups in town, and Jeff still works full-time as a teacher in our public school system! Cindy's whole family has also come back to the Lord. Her dad plays on our worship team, and her mom is a ministry leader. They were rescued from the abyss of bitterness! That is just one of many, many stories I could tell of how God is changing so many people's lives around us. For months now, we have been having a "Life Change Through Jesus" story every week, because there are so many people being radically changed.

QUESTIONS:

• Are you doing what God has put right in front of you with all your heart? What's holding you back?

• How can you set aside your fears, bitterness, and pain from the past?

We quickly outgrew that room, moved into a school, grew out of that, and moved into a community center that was pretty big. We had a big set-up too—30 foot rolls of carpet, 150 chairs, and walls made of canvas and PVC pipe! It took us about two hours to set up every Sunday, then I would go change in the bathroom. I met several new people coming to use the facilities while I was getting my "preacher pants" on! As soon as the service was over, back into shorts I went and tore the whole thing down and packed it into a 8 by 14 foot dual-axle trailer.

Our goal was not to build a church at that point, but a team to build the church. We wanted a team of people who loved God, loved each other, and by golly, loved the pastor! I used to say over and over. I always tell my church, "If you don't like me, **please** don't come to church here!"

It was a blessing to be able to build from the ground up, with people who had the same vision. Instead of my chasing after people who weren't happy, we would ask them to worship elsewhere. We still do this today. We **want** people to love church and be happy, so if they aren't, we help them find a place where they will be.

Within the first two years, God answered our prayers, and we had about 80 people who had our vision, loved each other, and loved us! Most of them are still leading with us or leading in another church somewhere in the Kingdom!

Then came the time for our five year goal: Influence in our city.

Soon before our fifth year anniversary, God gave us our first permanent facility and we really started to grow, not only in attendance, but in team. People began to come, get healed, and start serving, start ministries, and host and lead small groups. It was amazing.

We went to two services in that facility, which was our fourth, and we were soon packed out, especially the kids church rooms. Our workers came out looking like were suffering from post-traumatic stress disorder. I knew we needed more space. So we started praying over the suite next door which was occupied by a Karate studio. We asked God to grow them so much they had to move so we could have it! We laid our hands on the walls and prayed hard. What we didn't know was we were praying a prayer God didn't want to answer. Our prophetic dreamers started dreaming. We were moving; we were loading our stuff up. Someone was handing me a big ring of gold keys.

It was just honestly stressing me out!

One Wednesday, I was driving home about 1 p.m. God spoke to me, "Go see Pastor Phil at Vision of Hope down the street." I had heard they were building a new building and would be moving.

Now, I don't know if you do this, but I argue with God, like I know **anything** about what I am talking about. I said, "Well God, it's lunch time and pastors are never there at lunchtime." Lame, I know. He told me to go again. So I said, "God, I don't even know Phil. He doesn't come to any of the pastors stuff, so it would be weird for me to just stop in." I know, lame.

But God said, "GO!"

So I said, "But, God, now I'm almost home." Aren't our arguments with God totally stupid? But finally, when I realized I was not going to shake God, I turned the big 15-passenger van around and drove all the way back past our building two blocks down to Vision of Hope, right across from the main entrance to our airport, next to the Santa Maria Times. It was a great location.

I walked in and asked to talk to the pastor. To my surprise, he was just sitting there, waiting for me it seemed. Pastors are *never* there at lunchtime!

We chatted for a bit when he asked the inevitable, "So, what's up?" I stammered around a bit, and then finally told him I was interested in seeing what they would be doing with their building when they moved to their new one. He looked straight at me and said, "We're giving it to you." Just like that. "We have been praying for someone to come along to take it from us. If not, we have to tear this whole church out of here, a half-million dollars worth of build-in, and turn it back into a warehouse. We have been asking God to bring someone." Well, I was shocked and didn't know what to say. We had no money, and we still had a year and a half left on our commercial lease. You don't *ever* get out of a commercial lease.

As he gave me a tour of this huge facility, I started hyperventilating—room after room, youth rooms, storage out the wazoo, three entrances, and even a kitchen; on the other end, there was a commercial café open to the public! My head was spinning. So I asked when they would be moving. Two to three years? How long would it take me to get ready for this? "No," he said. "Four months." I was devastated. There was no way. I had a lease, no money, and not enough time for vision casting. Hmmmm …

He told me it was ours if we wanted it and said to let him know if we figured it out. I walked out to the van completely overwhelmed.

I hadn't even talked to Cindy to let her know I was stopping by, so I called and told her what had just happened—when I had a thought. My friend from a local Foursquare church had just got their building sold out from under them. They had been there 13 years and were now close to having to vacate. I called her and asked, "Do you want my building?"

Almost without pause she said, "Yes! I have always loved your building!"

God messed up my ducks. Now I live in a place I never knew existed but have always wanted to be.

So just like that, within an hour God had given us a new, big building and given ours away. To shorten the story here, our current landlord let the other church sign for the rest of our lease; we were able to come up with $60,000 to get into the new building and remodel it in 90 days end-to-end. We have now filled it twice over with two services each Sunday morning.

In these last years, God has done more than I could ever think, ask, or imagine. But it was all a result of a simple little spiritual gift assessment I did where God showed me that my faith was weak. With my permission, He messed up my ducks, and now I live in a place I never knew existed but have always wanted to be. I pastor the church I always wanted to go to, and we are seeing amazing results in the "influence" part of our vision in our city.

Cindy was the president of the PTA of Andrew's school of 1,000 kids for four years; I am on the school site council, have been on boards of non-profits, and worked in the Juvenile Detention Center. I am on the Block Grants Advisory Committee for the Mayor as a sworn member of our city government; Chaplain at Hardy Diagnostics, a company of about 200 employees; and President of the Santa Maria Valley Ministerial Association of over 90 churches— and that is just me. Our church is full of people that love to serve and reach out to the community. We send out groups on missions around the world and have a huge youth and college ministry called Generation Church. We run a recovery program, have nearly 30 small groups, and have tons of visitors every Sunday.

My heart beats for my city, my family, and this church God has placed me in. We are already raising up the next generation to take the ball from us and run. We have in our hearts internships, recording studios, preaching teams, multi-campuses, and ministries; the next generation is already taking us there!

I have a great staff, and a whole pastoral team of incredible people that love Church for Life as much as we do, including several apprentice teams training to be pastors. God has turned this bitter PK into a man whose heart beats for people ... yes, even *church* people! This scripture has been a favorite for me through this process.

When the people return to their homeland, they will remove every trace of their vile images and detestable idols. And I will give them singleness of heart and put a new spirit within them. I will take away their stony, stubborn heart and give them a tender, responsive heart, so they will obey my decrees and regulations. Then they will truly be my people, and I will be their God. But as for those who long for vile images and detestable idols, I will repay them fully for their sins. I, the Sovereign Lord, have spoken!

Ezekiel 11:18-21 (NLT)

Have some of your traumatic experiences become idols in your life? Have you elevated them above God or serving God? This might account for your hard heart.

Bottom line? You can do this, PK. You can make it through too. In the last chapters, I want to share with you some things I have learned along my way that may help you get through the **test** and on to your own **test**imony.

They overcame him by the blood of the Lamb and by the word of their testimony; they did not love their lives so much as to shrink from death.

Revelation 12:11 (NIV)

QUESTIONS:

• What impossible things has God made possible in your own life?

• For what does your heart beat?

• What is in your heart to do, dream for, or are you currently doing in your city?

These things that you went through growing up are not GOD'S fault. I want to bring it home for you. My hope is that God has softened your heart over the course of reading this book. I hope you realize you are not the only one who has been through this poop. I hope you recognize God can change **any** heart, including yours. Let's do this. Here's what I've learned that has led to my restoration and passion for people and The House of the Lord.

After doing this close to 20 years, I am always amazed at how many people blame God for the dysfunction caused by disobedience to God. That's the whole point; the reason that there is trauma and dysfunction is that it is the wages earned from disobeying God. I have had countless people sit in my office and cry, whine, and complain about the situation they are in or were put in, then direct the anger at God when what they were getting was a *fair* wage for their sin. Death has been the payment for sin since the fall in the Garden of Eden; it still is. It hasn't changed in thousands of years. Thank God, there is grace and forgiveness through Jesus Christ; but that takes admitting the truth about our part and participation. If you grew up in death, it wasn't because of God; it was because of people's unwillingness to turn to Him.

God *is* love; God *is* peace, God *is* restoration. If that was not your experience, someone was disobeying. When sin happened, God decided to let us go our own way and just have access to Him if we chose to. If we won't, then death will seep into everything and everyone around us.

You know, part of the reason both my brothers and I are serving God in full-time ministry is when we saw people who had split and left our church, our parents would make us smile and wave at them. We did this in the midst of all the dysfunction in the churches we grew up in. Dad would warn us, "Boys, wave as we go by, or I will spank you." He was communicating something to us: this is bigger than I am, and I don't have to participate. Although it ruined my dad and mom to this day, I think they planted something is us that has obviously produced a lot of fruit. I am attempting to plant that same seed in you right now, PK! So it's not God's fault, but this second one is equally important.

Would you pray with me?

God, we repent for holding You responsible for the dysfunction caused by man's disobedience. We realize You are a God of peace, joy, love, patience, kindness, faithfulness, gentleness and self-control. If those around us had exercised those things, we would not have had to walk through this death. We know You are not bound by this, but we are, and we release our attachment to this lie and break every tie we have to it. God, I believe You are not the Author of this kind of confusion, but you are the Author and Finisher of my faith.

*T**hese things that you went through growing up are not* *YOUR fault.* You know, as a PK, somewhere along the line, I began to take personal responsibility for all the negativity and dysfunction in my dad's church, like it was my fault this was happening. The greatest tool in Satan's arsenal is the lie, and he is good at selling it. Are you buying?

The old lady who taught Sunday school in the church I grew up in gave us a hard time for not being perfect because we were the pastor's kids. Then, she acted like the Devil himself towards my dad. Somehow, I connected those two things in my mind and began to think it was my fault. I was only an innocent bystander. When I went to that meeting where I saw my dad verbally beaten and accused, it seemed like there was something I should have done. I should have protected him. The truth is I should have **been** protected. To move on from this, you will have to release yourself from responsibility for it. I don't like the word *victim*; that can lead to pity parties. At most, you are an innocent bystander, a witness to a horrible accident caused by running the red light of God's principles. Take the load off; it's not your fault.

Jesus, I pray for a supernatural revelation and a supernatural release in this area of blame and personal responsibility. I break the lie that has been sold to me. Through the power of the Holy Spirit, I break the buying of that lie too. This is a prison I will not sit in. As a PK, I take the keys of the Truth and claim freedom. I know this freedom has to be accepted. Will you help me open my heart to accept this freedom and grace so generously and lavishly offered? I have personally received, and now I pray an impartation to be able to. In Jesus' name.

These things that you went through growing up are not DEVIL'S fault.

> **_People's desires_** make them give in to immoral ways, filthy thoughts, and shameful deeds.
> Galatians 5:19 (CEV) [emphasis added]

If we knew how little power Satan actually has over believers, it would shock most people. His power was broken through the cross!

> And having disarmed the powers and authorities, he made a public spectacle of them, triumphing over them by the cross.
> Colossians 2:15 (NIV)

We love to blame the Devil for all of this; it's just easier, but ultimately all he has is these tricky and powerful lies to sell. The scripture above is clear that it is "people's desires" that make them give in. Adam and Eve ate the apple; Satan didn't force feed it to them. But the first thing she did was blame him, and Adam blamed her. It's so easy to blame the Devil, but that won't set you free. The politics and religiousness that gets into the church are bought and brought there by people's desires to be top dog. If I had a penny for every person who has tried to use me as a pastor to get them to the top "position," I would have a pretty big penny jar! We make people coming from other churches, especially if they have been in ministry, sit back for **two years** and just absorb our DNA before placing them anywhere. This has been crucial to our ability to restore broken ministry families.

Let's put the responsibility where it lies—with people's desires for power.

We define maturity around Church for Life as "going from it's all about me to it's not about me at all!" Now that is a journey that we are **all** on!

Jesus, help me to quit blaming the Devil for what is clearly our buying into a lie. Satan has no power to make a believer greedy or power-hungry; it comes from somewhere way down deep in us. This has caused problems in our lives, in our churches, and in me. I break every lie that would misplace responsibility for the dysfunction and accept my part of responsibility of getting my life healed.

Caution, this is a tough one!

It's not God's fault, not your fault, and not Satan's fault; but **some** of it **is** your dad's fault (or mom's fault if she was the one in ministry).

This was the hardest part for me. I **wanted** my dad to be the hero. I **wanted** him to be the perfect one in this whole thing. I put blame everywhere and on everything but him. But the fact was … my dad was a poor leader at times. He was non-confrontational and let so many things go until they blew up. He chased people he should have cut loose. He let obvious things fester until it was cancerous. As much as I wanted to see him as the guy on the white horse with shining armor who had done nothing wrong, he just hadn't won. He wasn't the knight in shining armor, and he wasn't riding a white horse. A lot of the problems we had were from his not leading well.

Granted, the church "system" he pastored in positioned pastors for disaster. People run churches where the pastor was a hire and fire, and definitely not a shepherd but a puppet. They voted every year; if you even **tried** to lead or shake the boat, you just got voted out. These churches are pastor-killers. The only sheep in these kinds of churches are the pastor and his kids. Everyone is in charge. This was the epitome of "too many chiefs and not enough Indians." With all of that said, there were still a lot of things my dad could have done differently to solve some of these issues.

I remember the day someone actually laid some blame at my dad's feet. I got **mad** and defensive. He was the victim … right? It took me a while to see his responsibility in all of this. Even if there is no way to win in the system you are in, change the system, leave it … or blow it up. I am known for doing this in different organizations I have been involved in leading; that it is my motto. I learned this from watching my dad live in a failing system. It's still failing today; those churches are all dying out. On average, they have 18 people on a Sunday morning, with rarely any visitors. It's time to pull the plug, folks!

What I am trying to say is if you are going to get through this, you are going to have to get honest about who is **actually** to blame. We create our own hell sometimes. Yes, we have an Enemy that is after us 24/7/365, but **we** are the ones who give in and buy the lie. My dad pastored out of insecurity and ended up depressed, in a tent in the backyard. Looking out the window at that tent, I will never forget the feeling of sorrow in my stomach. He could have led better.

Disappointment is a killer. You become a personality addict. You want this person or that person to be your savior, but it doesn't happen. I have seen too many people ruined by disappointment in people, but we were never supposed to put our trust in people. We can trust people but not **place** our trust in people. We live disappointed this way. It took me **years** to replace that disappointment in my dad's failure with discipleship, following the **only** One who won't disappoint: Jesus. This is our only hope, PK.

At one point, I just had to get my eyes off people. This was Saul's problem. Saul always thought about how people perceived him, how people betrayed him, how people would take his "spot"— people, people, people—and it ruined him. He became a murderous, schizophrenic leader because he just couldn't see past people.

> Let us fix our eyes on Jesus, the author and perfecter of our faith ...
>
> Hebrews 12:2 (NIV)

So what do we do with all of this?

Cut our parents some slack. It was what it was, and as long as we are being honest about it, God can bring us His grace to release it. After all, we will make our own set of mistakes, maybe different ones, but mistakes nonetheless. We will need that same grace offered to us by our children someday. If you want that later, sow the seed for it now. This can build you if you don't let it break you. Read on.

Jesus, this is really hard to admit, but the people that I NEEDED to be my heroes failed me at times. They weren't perfect, and I wanted them to be. They were supposed to be on a pedestal that You needed to be on; I replaced You with them. With this realization, I offer the same grace to them that You have given me—Your supernatural grace, poured through me, right into their lives. I want to be part of their healing, and I believe that as I step into health, there will be a new level of my parents' stepping into health, and I want to be a part of that. Holy Spirit, I am asking for a restoration of my innocence, and a restoration of my trust in the ultimate leader, Jesus Christ. I now release my parents from the weight of not being the perfect pastors. I redirect that trust that I tried to put in them to you right now. In Jesus' name.

This is where we begin to actually turn from *me*-focused heal-ing to people who are commissioned, focused, and produc-ing. I believe there is nothing as fun and fulfilling as changing the world! This was the big shift for me. When I realized this, the experience I had walked through growing up was *not* a liability; it was an asset!

I see people with stars in their eyes wanting to be "that guy" on the stage—the "Pastor"— and I realize they have no idea what it means. I realize this could be the reason the average tenure of a pastor is less than two years. Seven out of ten church plants fail. This position corrupts people at such high rates. People just don't know what the life of a pastor is like.

But we do! We know exactly what we are getting into when we accept this commission. We know what to expect. PK, if you will walk through this healing, you will be so far ahead of most in your qualifications because of the revelations!

When I realized all I had been through and had to process grow-ing up had *been* the training and discipleship they can't teach in seminary, I began to see this as *not* a liability but a *great* asset! There have been eight church plants in our city since we planted. Only two of us are really thriving. Several have disbanded, many are just maintaining after just a few years, and most of these guys have seminary training and have been through church planting "boot camps." I can honestly say I think the best training in the world is growing up in a pastor's home, fighting all of these expectation battles *before* launching instead of trying to do that in the middle of pastoring people.

Our current kids' church coordinator lives with us. She is a 21-year-old woman full of fire and passion. I think she has learned more by living with us than she could have learned in some seminaries. Everyday is a new revelation and a new wrestling match. You can't buy this kind of training! PK, you are primed and trained for greatness by what you have seen and lived through. Like Saul/Paul in the New Testament, turn hate and disappointment into directed and managed passion for the King! He didn't do this to try to ruin you; He put you in one of the best schools in the world—the school of the PK home! Turn it from a liability into an asset. I have, and man, does it work for me!

Jesus, I simply don't like training, and You KNOW I hate tests; but this word "disciple" has a lot behind it. I confess in faith right now, I have been prepared for greatness by being a PK. This WAS my training. This WILL add to any other training and degree I will ever get. I turn my perspective right now from my past's being a liability to being one of the greatest assets of my life. In fact, right now, Lord, in faith, I am going to thank You for placing me in a pastor's home. I thank you for the privilege of this level and quality of training and discipleship. Help me now to step all the way through this to full healing so I can put all this training to use for Your Kingdom. I'm going to change the world!

N ow we will redirect our focus from past to future, turning from what was to what is and will be—turning focus from me … to my generation, like Noah, Daniel, Gideon, Joseph, Moses, Joshua, Stephen, Peter, and Paul did. I can change the world, **but I must get healed before I do, or the world will change me**.

In the next five chapters are five things I have learned about healing.

> *Jesus replied, "Blessed are you, Simon son of Jonah, for this was not revealed to you by flesh and blood, but by my Father in heaven. And I tell you that you are Peter, and on this rock I will build my church, and the gates of Hades will not overcome it."*
>
> *Matthew 16:17-18 (NIV)*

This kind of deep stuff can't be just "learned." Even this book can only open your heart to the big "T" Teacher, or *Rabboni*, as Mary called Him in the garden (John 20:16). When I speak on this stuff, people want to come tell me *their* stories, have *me* pray for them, and get an impartation from me. That's all good, and I'm glad to do it; but the *real* revelation is going to come from the Father.

My purpose in this book is to simply build your faith to go the Father—the Counselor and Healer. Up in Lincoln, Montana, in the middle of the mountains at a men's retreat, I was wrestling it out with God. No one else even knew life change was happening in me that weekend. I was at the tipping point. I was either going to accept this destiny or walk away never to discuss it again. There was no person who could have walked me through that, but the person of Jesus and the power of His Holy Spirit. As much as I would like to say there is a formula for this, you will need some personal revelations. This will require humbling yourself, turning from sin, and sitting at the cross where He made it possible for us to step into His incredible, lavish love. It's *all* available, but only *you* can go get it for yourself.

Jesus, I come to you right now. I come to the cross with my big sack of junk. I know it's all garbage, but I can't seem to get rid of it. I need a personal revelation of who You are. In faith, I humble myself before You as my Teacher and Savior. This is not optional; I need a transformed mind. I believe it will come through a revelation of who You are, what You do, and what You will do in me and through me. With the right revelation, I can change the world.

In working with addicted people, bitter people, damaged people, and hurt people, I have come to see something clearly. The people who don't get better always have at least *one* thing holding them back—one excuse ... lame excuses even. One guy won't go to our weekly recovery program or go off to a recovery program because he will miss visits with his son, although he is so stoned, he misses most visits with his son anyway. Everyone has an excuse of why to not move on. Get this PK: you will never move past the line you have drawn by using your excuses. That is where you will stop. It is time to blow up the excuses and make a decision for change. Behind that one decision flows the tremendous grace of God.

Maturity is going from it's all about me, to it's not about me at all; this is the decision it will take to move in to be and feel healthy. The rich young ruler had an invitation to be personally discipled by Jesus, but with one decision walked away from his destiny (Mark 10:17). I see so many people do this on a regular basis, then they look back and wonder what happened to that dream for their lives.

> *"One thing you lack," [the one thing that will hold you back]*
> *... "Go, sell everything you have and give to the poor, and*
> *you will have treasure in heaven. Then come, follow me."* 22
> *At this the man's **face fell**. He went away sad, because he*
> *had great wealth.*
>
> Mark 10:21-22 (NIV) [emphasis added]

Jesus went right for this young man's main excuse—the main thing that would hold him back—and that is what He will do with you, PK. There are millions of us not serving God, living sad, unfulfilled, lonely lives because of the one thing that holds us back.

Will you let God at it? This is the decision.

This young guy wanted it ... just on his own terms.

The big decision will be to go to God on His terms and give up the idols of hate, regret and disappointment that, technically, you have elevated above God in your life.

I **know** it hurt! I know. I know. I feel it because I was the one up there losing it at the altar while my dad got thrown to the wolves behind me, and I did nothing. I feel you; but it's time to end the excuse. Move into "it's not about you" maturity. You can do it; it will just require a bold decision on your part.

Jesus, will You just blow up my excuse right now? I have drawn so many lines this way, and I am ready to stop. Unlike the rich kid, I want to take You up on Your offer. I want to sell the most important thing to me to get out from under it. I need You to show me what it is by asking me sell it, or get rid of it. I will say "yes," no matter how valuable it is to me. I want the next level on Your terms.

There was another man in the Bible who had an opportunity with Jesus, yet with all of his passion, everyone was trying to keep him down and keep him quiet, keeping him from moving forward. His name was Blind Bartimaeus (Mark10:46-52). The moment he tried to get free, people started telling him to shut up, be still, go away, and that it was no use. PK, one thing I need to warn you about here is the old adage "birds of a feather flock together." This means most likely you have surrounded yourself with people with the same hurts as your own. It's our default. We surround ourselves with people struggling with the same stuff so we can normalize it. The problem with that is when you go to change, they will fight you, discourage you, and maybe even try and sabotage you.

Why? Because if *you* change, they won't have an excuse of why *they* can't change too!

I saw this over and over at the car dealership with guys who were trying to quit smoking. As soon as a guy tried to quit, everybody in the place would begin to offer him cigarettes until he caved. One guy even said, "I will not buy anymore cigarettes, period. But I will smoke one here and there if someone offers one to me." What happened? He probably smoked more than he did before. Those guys weren't going to let him quit, because then they would feel the pressure or conviction to do it too. Be warned. When you start getting healthy, it will bring out all the insecurities of the people you have potentially surrounded yourself with; they will try and pull you back in. It may even come from some place you didn't expect. My own dad discouraged me from going into full-time ministry because of his own experience. You have to push through. This will take determination. This will take the power of the Holy Spirit. If Blind Bart can press through the negativity of the crowd, so can you.

Jesus, I block my ears to the naysayers and the people I have surrounded myself with who would want to keep me bummed out. I will push through the crowd. I am willing to fall in front of people. I am willing to be seen as weak. I am willing to call attention to my handicaps in order to get to You for healing. I will see again. Vision is coming; I call it in by faith.

If true faith is believing something good you can't see (yet), then believing in something **bad** you can't see (yet) is negative faith. I introduced this idea at the beginning of the book, but it is worth repeating. I can't believe how much negative faith is going around today, even in the Church. I contend that this faith is just about as strong in our lives as true faith is, which is positive, good news! Behind true faith is the power of God's spirit, but behind negative faith is every demonic power of Satan. He thrives on negativity!

Our first step of action here is to go from negative faith to true, positive faith; from believing the worst in people and situations, to believing the best; from believing the worst in yourself and your situation, to believing the best! This is where life changed for me. A major part of this revelation came from my wonderful wife, Cindy. Link yourself up with healthy people who have what you don't; these people can impart something and will tell you the truth about you!

Action will engage the gears of everything God has waiting for you. You just have to start! Start with an appointment with somebody! Start speaking faith like, "I am going to get to the next level; it's right in front of me. I am leaving all that behind. I like people who love the church. *I* love the church. I love Jesus, and if the church is His bride, then I am going to love His wife!" You start commanding what your mouth **says** instead of your mouth commanding what your heart **feels.** No one can take action for you. **You** have to take action. Go to a conference; go to a pastor; go reconcile with someone.

DO SOMETHING! It's the only way to get something done!

Holy Spirit, I need Your help to take the next step. I believe You love me and want to bless me. I am switching directions from negative faith to TRUE faith, which is positive, believing the best in people, in Your church, and in authority. Will You place some great people around me who have things I don't have who can impart these things to me? I am taking action!

M ost people who will ever live, throughout all of history, will live in the default—the path of least resistance. Remember, just like electricity will always flow in this path of least resistance, most people will spend their whole lives there too, living for themselves, stealing, lying, hating, abusing, and looking out only for their own interests. Bad marriages are the norm. Finances in chaos are the norm. Complaining at work everyday is the norm.

Then, all of a sudden, you find someone different, someone who refuses to travel in the bottom of the rut. That someone decides to swim upstream and will give his or her life for another.

We call these heroes.

As a youth pastor for 10 years, I called them culture climbers. We would come across these kids who, instead of smoking pot behind the stadium bleachers, would go and set up their band in the public school hallways and play worship during lunch. A hundred kids would gather around, worshipping right there on the school campus. These are interesting people. Some of these kids are now pastors, missionaries, and now, some of these "kids" are pastoring with us here in California. I believe against the odds of the default; I **can** change my generation. I can be a culture climber, rising to the top of my generation. I don't just want to pastor in this city; I love being the president of the my city's ministerial association influencing nearly 100 pastors in my city. Why **not** climb to the top?

If you don't believe this is possible, I challenge you to go and begin to read the story of Esther, Moses, Noah, David, Gideon, Joshua, Daniel, and more recently the disciples, Peter, Paul, and on and on. All these people left an imprint on history and their generations. I believe this is still possible today. The way you process and handle this thing called "LIFE" from this day forward is adjusting generations way down the line. Your actions are affecting hundreds, if not thousands, **right now**. Now is the best time to make some good decisions!

You see, throughout the Old Testament, one generation served God, then the next didn't. They got some discipline, came back a few generations later, then it happened again. The next generation had no knowledge of the great things God did to save and protect their grandparents and great-grandparents. We have a great responsibility to provide a connection or, better yet, **be** the connection between the great things God has done for us. We are also responsible for the communication and passing of that knowledge to the next generations.

If you will choose, like I did, to learn some of the same things discussed over the past few chapters, there will be thousands that will be blessed because of it. See, my dad grew up in a very dysfunctional home, but he gave his life to the Lord and ended that dysfunction with **his** generation. Part of our calling and destiny is to end the drama, pass on blessing, climb to the top of **our** current generation, and change the world.

PK, you have been specially trained to do this. I am; will you join me?

chapter

a passionate prayer for pk's

Now that you've read this book and we've connected our hearts through our stories, let me just take a moment to pray with you. This is my prayer; will you join me?

Our Father in Heaven, Your name is awesome! Your Word says that just the mention of Your name has power. Now I call on that Name, that power for the healing and regeneration of my heart. In the name of Jesus, I pray that You would replace our kingdom built of opinions, hurt, lies and pressures with Your Kingdom of Peace.

I am asking that Your Kingdom would come, but, more importantly, that we would be obedient so Your will would be done—not necessarily done like I want it done, but done here, right now on earth, just like it is done in Heaven. We KNOW how it is done in Heaven—just exactly like You want it done! That is the same atmosphere we want in our own lives and the kingdoms we are building here on earth. Invade the religiousness and hypocrisy that we have seen, and, like Jericho, tear it apart for a BETTER kingdom established and built by the Good Shepherd. However, like Rahab, I'm asking this:

In the tearing down of that Kingdom ... spare me! Spare my heart! Do not let me be so attached to those feelings that I crumble with the old kingdoms' walls! I set out my faith right now as that red cord ... disconnect my destiny from the dysfunction of the old way of thinking.

Will You right now give me what I need for today? I need to live fresh for today, to have strength to lift bitterness and past ways of thinking, and to blow up all expectations that are not Yours.

This will be my daily sustenance, my daily bread. Not only do I pray for provision, but I also ask for prosperity. Where I have more than enough, let the cup of my life run over to those around me.

As I look at Your unlimited grace and forgiveness, I pray that I would have that same grace and forgiveness for those around me. Would You pour out that grace and forgiveness on me for the ways I have been acting and thinking? Moreover, would You give ME the grace to pour it out on those who have wronged me? As You forgive my debts, help me to forgive the debts of those around me.

Lead me now away from temptation, deliver me from future evils, and expose every lie and scheme of my enemies. This will be to Your honor, Your glory, and Your Kingdom forever and ever. Amen.

Made in the USA
Lexington, KY
12 January 2012